Gary L. Harbaugh, Ph.D., is a licensed psychologist, pastoral consultant, and widely known workshop leader. Dr. Harbaugh has an interdisciplinary degree from the University of Chicago and graduated from the clinical psychology postdoctoral program of the School of Professional Psychology, Wright State University. He has served congregations in Ohio, Illinois, Massachusetts, and Florida and currently teaches pastoral care and psychology at Trinity Lutheran Seminary. He is a faculty member in the MBTI Training Program of the Association for Psychological Type (APT) and is on the consulting faculty of the Center for Applications of Psychological Type (CAPT). Dr. Harbaugh is also a psychological consultant for the Division for Ministry of the Evangelical Lutheran Church in America, the founder of Kairos Care and Counseling,^{SM} and the coordinator of an interprofessional counseling support program for persons in full-time ministry and their families, with service centers in Florida and Ohio. Dr. Harbaugh can be reached at Trinity Lutheran Seminary, 2199 E. Main St., Columbus OH 43209.

"God's Gifted People is a practical guide that can help persons identify, nurture, and strengthen their gifts. . . . This book has given me a fresh, new way of working with giftedness, both personally and in the congregational setting."

Clyde C. Fry, past president
Academy of Parish Clergy

GOD'S GIFTED PEOPLE

"Having gifts that differ
according to the
grace given to us,
let us use them"

Romans 12:6

GOD'S GIFTED PEOPLE

EXPANDED EDITION

*Discovering Your
Personality
as a Gift*

Gary L. Harbaugh

AUGSBURG ■ MINNEAPOLIS

GOD'S GIFTED PEOPLE
Discovering Your Personality as a Gift
Expanded Edition

Scripture quotations unless otherwise noted are from the Revised Standard Version of the Bible, copyright 1946, 1952, and 1971 by the Division of Christian Education of the National Council of Churches.

Material by Gordon Lawrence from *People Types and Tiger Stripes: A Practical Guide to Learning Styles*, 2nd ed. (Gainesville, FL: Center for Applications of Psychological Type, 1979, 1982), is used by permission of Gordon Lawrence.

Material by Isabel Briggs Myers from *Introduction to Type* (Palo Alto, CA; Consulting Psychologists Press, 1962, 1987) is reproduced by special permission of the publisher, Consulting Psychologists Press, Inc., 577 College Ave., Palo Alto CA 94306.

The chorus of "A Place in the Choir" by Bill Staines, © 1978 Mineral River Music Co., Box 292, Dover NH 03820, is used by permission.

Cover design: Terry Dugan

Library of Congress Cataloging-in-Publication Data

Harbaugh, Gary L., 1936–
   God's gifted people : discovering your personality as a gift /
Gary L. Harbaugh. — Expanded ed.
     p.   cm.
   Includes bibliographical references.
   ISBN 0-8066-2486-8 (alk. paper)
   1. Gifts, Spiritual. 2. Personality—Religious aspects—
Christianity. 3. Christian life—1960–   4. Myers–Briggs Type
Indicator. I. Title.
BT767.3.H35   1990
234′.13—dc20   90-35515
                                                      CIP

The paper used in this publication meets the minimum requirements of American National Standard for Information Sciences—Permanence of Paper for Printed Library Materials, ANSI Z329.48-1984. ∞™

Manufactured in the U.S.A.   AF 9-2486
94   93   92   91   90   1   2   3   4   5   6   7   8   9   10

Contents

Preface		8
1	What Does the Bible Say about Gifts of the Spirit?	11
2	What Kinds of Personality Gifts Are There?	18
3	The Gift of Practicality: Living in the Here and Now	33
4	The Gift of Personal Helpfulness: Reaching Out and Lifting Up	49
5	The Gift of Possibilities for People: Keeping Hope Alive	61
6	The Gift of Looking Ahead: Letting the Future Guide the Present	73
7	"Having Gifts That Differ ... Let Us Use Them"	88
References and Resources		107
How to Use This Book: Applications for Personal Growth		112
Index		143

Preface

This is a book about gifts from God. What I have to say about these gifts comes out of my personal experience and Christian faith. Many of the ideas are applicable to those of other faiths, and I invite those of you who can do so to make the specific connections. Whether a deep religious commitment guides your life or not, my hope is that you will find in these pages a positive and helpful way of looking at life and at other people.

This book is meant to help you discover or learn more about one of God's very special gifts, a gift you may have overlooked—the gift expressed through your unique personality. If you already know how you have been gifted, this book may help you to use your gifts more effectively or more faithfully. Even if you believe you are using your gifts effectively at the present time, I encourage you to keep reading. Most of the people I know are much more gifted than they realize. They are using only part of their gift. Perhaps you have been given more than you have recognized. This book may help you tap into your unused potential.

Your gift is meant to be used in a particular way. Passages from the Bible tell us that we are all gifted in some way. We are also to use our diverse gifts for a common goal: "to equip the saints for the work of ministry, for building up the body of Christ" (Eph. 4:7-12). While the Ephesians passage certainly refers to how we use God's gifts in the church, it goes far beyond that. When we read the word *saints* it is understandable that we start to get images in our mind of great persons of faith. However, if you have a husband or a wife, a son or a daughter, parents, or some other significant person in your life, remember that they are included among God's saints. Your God-given gifts are not only to be used in the congregation, but also at home with your family. When you use your gifts at home, then, you are "equipping the saints" just as much as when you teach a Sunday school class or attend an important church conference.

We are also to use our gift for the work of ministry. In the Bible, the work of ministry does not only mean *ordained* ministry. *Every* Christian has a calling, a vocation, and that is his or her ministry. Christians are to use their gifts in the fulfillment of their calling, no matter what that calling might be. When we, with Christ in mind, use our talents in ways that contribute to the welfare of any of God's people, then we are doing "the work of ministry."

Of course, a very special place for the stewardship of our gifts is in our local congregations. The Bible tells us that the church is Christ's body and that we are to use our gift "for building up the body of Christ." To be a good steward is an ongoing challenge for every Christian. But if we are to be good stewards, we must know what it is we have to contribute.

You are one of God's gifted people. What are your gifts and, especially, what is your *personality* gift? How can it be best used at home, at work, and in the church? As Bill Staines has pointed out in a delightful song entitled "A Place in the Choir," "all God's critters got a place in the choir, some sing low and some sing higher, some sing out loud on the telephone wire and some just clap their hands or paws. . . ." The "choir," of course, is God's world, and whether we "sing low" or "sing higher" or just clap our hands, Staines is reminding us that every person has something to contribute. We all have a place in God's grand design. What is *your* place? What good does God intend to come to others through you? These are questions this book will help you answer. Above all, may this book help you appreciate even more how God has, through the diversity of gifts, richly blessed us all.

Preface

God's Gifted People has been made easier to read and potentially more useful because a number of people, carefully selected to represent each of the personality gifts included in the book, took an advance look at what I wrote and offered their suggestions. I appreciate the contributions of those who in this way shared their gifts: William Beckwith, Rebecca Brenneis, Eugene Dahnke, Loxi Dailey, Dr. Merlin Hoops, Robert Moluf, Andy Neugebauer, Dr. James Schaaf, Roland Seboldt, Dr. Trygve Skarsten, Linda Hume Skelly, and Chandler Tyrrell.

At the Center for Applications of Psychological Type, both Dr. Mary H. McCaulley and Jamelyn DeLong offered encouragement and support, as did Dr. Allen Hammer and Lorin Letendre of Consulting Psychologists Press (CPP gave permission for my use of *Introduction to Type*). Also helpful were my APT MBTI Training Program faculty colleagues. One of them, Dr. Gordon Lawrence, graciously allowed me to make use of a portion of his book, *People Types and Tiger Stripes*.

Too many to name, but too important to overlook, I have learned much from those who have participated in my courses and workshops on the Myers–Briggs and Ministry, and also from my able editors at Augsburg.

In addition, I am always enlightened by the insights of my wife, Marlene. Because her gifts are very different from mine, our life together has shown me firsthand how the diversity of God's gifts enables God's people to experience the breadth and depth of life much more fully.

To all of these gifted people, my thanks.

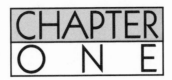

CHAPTER ONE

What Does the Bible Say about Gifts of the Spirit?

The Bible has much to say about gifts. Most of it is implicit. For example, even though the Bible does not say in so many words that King David was a gifted leader of the people of Israel, all of us would recognize that one of David's gifts was the gift of leadership. Similarly, nowhere does the Bible say that Paul was a gifted evangelist, yet we all know that one of Paul's gifts was the gift of winning persons to Christ.

But the Bible is crystal clear about the fact that each Christian is gifted in a special way. The best-known passages are found in Ephesians 4, Romans 12, 1 Corinthians 12, and 1 Peter 4, but I think the proper place to begin is with John 3:16: "For God so loved the world. . . ." John 3:16 is a reminder that, whenever we are thinking about gifts, Christians should remember who is the Source of all gifts, and how, in Christ, God has given us the greatest gift of all. In the giving of the Son, even to death on a cross, we know the love of God, who withholds from us nothing that we truly need. Keep the Giver in mind as we look further at what the Bible says about gifts.

Ephesians 4:7, 11-12

One of the primary passages that tells us about our giftedness is the passage from Ephesians that we quoted earlier, Eph. 4:7,11-12:

> But grace was given to each of us according to the measure of Christ's gift.
>
> And his gifts were that some should be apostles, some prophets, some evangelists, some pastors and teachers, to equip the saints for the work of ministry, for building up the body of Christ.

There are some key phrases in these verses that should be noted. The first is "to each of us." Some of God's gifts come to every Christian, such as the gift of God's Son or the gift of baptism or the gift of justification by grace. But other gifts are very personal and individual. "To each of us" balances those gifts that come to all of us with the special gift God gives to each individual person. In Ephesians this personal gift is linked with a gift of grace from Christ.

The Ephesians passage also says, "according to the measure of Christ's gift." The word *measure* in English is associated with quantity (how *much* of a gift). But the Greek word in Ephesians from which "measure" is translated accents the diversity of gifts given by God.

What follows in the passage is a list of different kinds of gifts, expressed in specific roles such as being a prophet or being a pastor and teacher. But notice that, even though the roles are different, they all exist for the same purpose: to equip the saints to do the work of ministry, to build up the body of Christ. (Biblical scholars point out that the Greek text does not require putting a comma after the word "saints." The saints are to be equipped for the work of ministry.) The point of these verses is that whatever the gift and whatever the role we play in life, each of us has been given a gift that is to be used for one and the same God-pleasing purpose.

Romans 12:1-8

A second passage communicates a similar message, although it is different in one important way. In the twelfth chapter of his letter to the Christians in Rome, Paul wrote:

> I appeal to you therefore ... by the mercies of God, to present your bodies as a living sacrifice, holy and acceptable to God, which is your spiritual worship. Do not be conformed to this world but be transformed by the renewal of your mind, that you may prove what is the will of God, what is good and acceptable and perfect.
>
> For by the grace given to me I bid every one among you not to think of [yourself] more highly than [you] ought to think, but to think with sober judgment, each according to the measure of faith which God has assigned.... For as in one body we have many members, and all the members do not have the same function, so we, though many, are one body in Christ, and individually members one of another. Having gifts that differ according to the grace given to us, let us use them: if prophecy, in proportion to our faith; if service, in our serving; [the one] who teaches, in teaching; [the one] who exhorts, in [the] exhortation; [the one] who contributes, in liberality; [the one] who gives aid, with zeal; [the one] who does acts of mercy, with cheerfulness.

Like Ephesians 4, Romans 12 is addressed both to a community and to individuals. The *community* is emphasized by the use of the word "we" and the references to the body as a whole, but the individual is highlighted in the address to "every one of you" and to the identification of the differing gifts that individuals have received. Paul went on to specify these "gifts that differ," not as Ephesians 4 does, in terms of formal roles, but in terms of different applications or ministries such as prophecy, service, teaching, exhortation, contribution, aid-giving, and acts of mercy. While prophecy might more typically come from someone recognized as a prophet, the book of Romans suggests that Christians in *all* walks of life may have been gifted in one or another of these ways.

Note carefully that the Romans passage does not say that any one person has *all* the gifts. New Testament professor Merlin Hoops once said to me that "the only one who has all the gifts is the one who was crucified. That none of us has all the gifts is a sign that we really are in this all together and we need each other." Therefore in the book of Romans we read what we also read in Ephesians, that we are not all gifted in the same way. We have different gifts. However, whatever our individual gift happens to be, we are encouraged to *use* that gift: "Having therefore gifts differing, let us use them" (v. 6, King James Version).

1 Corinthians 12:1-12

Another passage that puts our gifts in proper perspective is what Paul wrote to the Christians in Corinth:

Now concerning spiritual gifts ... I do not want you to be uninformed ...

Now there are varieties of gifts, but the same Spirit; and there are varieties of service, but the same Lord; and there are varieties of working, but it is the same God who inspires them all in every one. To each is given the manifestation of the Spirit for the common good. To one is given through the Spirit the utterance of wisdom, and to another the utterance of knowledge according to the same Spirit, to another faith by the same Spirit, to another gifts of healing by the one Spirit, to another the working of miracles, to another prophecy, to another the ability to distinguish between spirits, to another various kinds of tongues, to another the interpretation of tongues. All these are inspired by one and the same Spirit, who apportions to each one individually as [the Spirit] wills.

For just as the body is one and has many members, and all the members of the body, though many, are one body, so it is with Christ.

In this passage Paul was trying to make sure that his readers were not confused about spiritual gifts. First, he clarified that the primary focus is not to be on the gift, but rather on the *Giver*. There are varieties of gifts, varieties of service, varieties of working. But it is the same Spirit, the same Lord, the same God who inspires them all. God is our unity, our common center. From the one God proceeds a variety of manifestations of the Spirit that take distinctive shape in different individuals. In one it takes the shape of wisdom, in another the shape of knowledge, or faith, or gifts of healing, or the working of miracles, or prophecy, or distinguishing between spirits, or tongues, or the interpretation of tongues. These gifts are apportioned to us on an individual basis, as God wills, but—as we found in the Ephesians passage—for a single purpose. Whatever the gift, it is to be used for the "common good" and to lead toward the unity of the body of Christ.

1 Peter 4:10-11

Finally, let us look at a passage from 1 Peter:

As each has received a gift, employ it for one another, as good stewards of God's varied grace: whoever speaks, as one who utters oracles of God; whoever renders service, as one who renders it by the strength which God supplies; in order that in everything God may be glorified through Jesus Christ. To him belong glory and dominion for ever and ever. Amen.

Once again we find the theme of individual gifts being used for the common good. God's grace is varied and individuals are given particular gifts so they can make needed contributions to the believing community. To do so is identified as good stewardship. But 1 Peter goes even further to say that, in the use of our gift, the gift should lead those with whom we share it not to us, but to the one who gave it to us. This is similar to what Jesus said in Matt. 5:16, that we are to let our light so shine that when others see what we do, they glorify God. The use of our gift is to point those who receive that gift to the Giver. Therefore if our gift is speaking, it should be clear to our hearers that we are God's oracle. If our gift is serving, it should be made known that our service is possible because of our being empowered by God. Our individual gifts have a purpose beyond *them*selves, and beyond *our*-selves. Our gift is to point to the Giver of all gifts in order that "in everything God may be glorified through Jesus Christ" (v. 11).

In summarizing the content of these passages, three themes should be underscored: (1) God is the Giver of gifts; (2) each individual person is in some way gifted by God; and (3) the purpose of any individual gift always goes beyond the individual, since it is to be used for the community, for the upbuilding of the church, and for the work of ministry to all people.

But before we can fully use God's gifts in the way that God intends, we must understand what our particular gifts are. Since God gives gifts not simply in the abstract, but to individual persons, it will be helpful for us to understand as much as we can about ourselves as individuals so we can see how it is that God might want to use us.

When I look at myself with this view of my giftedness in mind, I am also aware of my limitations and failings. God intends me to use my gifts freely for others, but I

may do so only reluctantly. With the apostle Paul, sometimes I just don't understand myself (Rom. 7:15-23). The
good that I would like to do very often ends up not getting
done, and that which I know it is not right to do is too
often the very thing I end up doing. When Karl Menninger
wrote a book some years ago entitled *Whatever Became
of Sin?*, my response was that if he had only asked me,
I could have told him. Sin has never seemed that far away
from me.

But sin does not have the final word. We who have
"died with Christ" are no longer slaves to sin. We can be
witnesses because by the power of God we have been
brought "from death to life" (Rom. 6:6-14). It is in this
power that the same apostle who wrote Romans 6 and 7
could also write Romans 12. Paul knew very well that we
are imperfect channels for God's grace. Yet God has chosen us, imperfections and all, to pass on the gifts that we
have been given—even as we pray that we might share
those gifts ever more faithfully.

One of the assumptions that lies behind this book is
that in the giving of a particular gift to a particular person,
God takes the whole person into consideration. What
makes my serving different from someone else's serving
is that my service comes through *me*, it is expressed
through my "personhood." My personhood includes my
personal history, my life situation, and my past and present
struggles. No one else can give precisely what I do, because, in giving me a gift, God has called me to use my
unique personhood in the passing on of that gift to others.
What we shall now consider more completely is the way
in which our individual personalities are, in a very special
way, the bearers of our gifts from God.

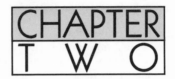

CHAPTER TWO

What Kinds of Personality Gifts Are There?

While one can talk about personality gifts in general, it is easier to think about them in relation to specific persons. In this book you will meet a number of people. Each one is unique, but each one is also the type of person who might live next door to you or who might attend your home congregation. As you read about them, you might think of other people you know who share their interests and concerns—and who might also share some of their very special gifts.

First you will meet a couple, Mike and Ellen.* Mike and Ellen have been married for 18 years. They moved to Fairvue when Mike was promoted after being named "Office Manager of the Year" at the marketing firm where he works. Mike is an outgoing person, quick to strike up a conversation with just about anyone. He appreciates employees who are good at what they do, and the fact that

---

*While the characters and situations in this book are true-to-life, the book is not about actual persons and no identification with actual persons is intended or should be inferred.

he rewards such staff members with regular raises and cost of living adjustments contributes to his popularity at work. The key to his success as a manager is his genuine belief that good management requires that the employer set an example for the employees, not expecting any more of an employee than the employer is willing to do. This conviction, combined with his fairness, makes Mike hard to beat as a boss.

Ellen is very different from her husband in many ways. Where Mike has many friends, Ellen has only a few persons that she would really call friends. She does not usually initiate conversations with people she does not already know, although she is friendly enough if someone approaches her first. While Ellen admires Mike's comfortableness in social situations and his success in his work, the last thing in the world she would want to do is have a job that involved selling.

There are other differences between Mike and Ellen which sometimes are apparent in their approach to raising their son. Mike is the organized one. He sets schedules and lives by deadlines, which works very well at the office. However, Ellen thinks that children need a more flexible environment if they are ever to learn to adapt to a changing world. She is widely read and sometimes wonders if Mike's desire for order in the home won't stifle the creativity that she has discovered in Andy, their son. Ellen would much prefer that Andy be sent to the experimental junior high school across town, where innovative teaching methods are used. However, Mike is afraid that if Andy misses out on the basics he will have a hard time in high school, as Mike himself did.

The personality differences between Mike and Ellen also show up in their relationship to the church. Soon after they moved to Fairvue five years ago, Mike and Ellen joined a church in their neighborhood. Mike felt attracted to the congregation because the service had a definite structure to it and the pastor appeared to be a good time manager, making sure that the worship hour lasted no longer than 60 minutes. Ellen also noticed that the service ran smoothly, but what really interested her was the quality of the Christian education program, not only for Andy but also for herself.

One Sunday after Mike and Ellen joined the church and Ellen began teaching the adult class, the topic in that class was the gifts of the Spirit. In a moment of uncharacteristic personal sharing, Ellen commented on how different she and Mike were and then raised a question about whether there might be a connection between certain personalities and specific spiritual gifts. Could it be, Ellen wondered, that God gives each person not only certain talents but also the gift of a particular personality through which that individual can express, in a unique and special way, the gifts of the Spirit?

In discussing gifts it is indeed possible to integrate psychological insight with theological understanding. One psychological theory that can be used is based on the work of Carl Gustav Jung, the son of an evangelical pastor in Switzerland. Among his many other publications, Jung wrote a book called *Psychological Types*. In that book he suggested that every person has an innate predisposition to develop certain personality characteristics. Put more simply, Jung believed that if our early family environment accepts us as we are and doesn't try too hard to change us, then our personality naturally develops in a particular direction. For example, Jung would say that Mike seems to have the kind of personality that just naturally moves outward toward the external world. He is active, outgoing, and practical. Mike also likes clear guidelines, and he is most comfortable working in a situation with definite boundaries. On the other hand, Ellen was born with a more reflective nature. Her inquiring mind, flexibility, and openness to new ideas make her a good student and an even better teacher.

While Jung described personality types in a purely psychological way, there is another way that Christians can look at these "innate predispositions." When a Christian considers the possibility that he or she was born with a personality gift, we cannot help but ask where the gift comes from. In other words, we look beyond the gift to the Giver.

In Psalm 139, we are given a powerful image of a God who knows us better than we know ourselves, a God who personally shapes us as individuals according to the Lord's own designs: "For thou didst form my inmost parts, thou didst knit me together in my mother's womb" (v. 13). What a wonderful image this is! In his book *Psalms for So-journers* (Augsburg, 1986), James Limburg tells the story of how he watched his mother-in-law knit a Norwegian sweater for each of the six members of his family. He marveled at her handiwork and the beautiful and useful results. Then it occurred to him that as difficult as it is to knit a Norwegian sweater, how much more complicated it is to knit a Norwegian! Or an American! Or you! Or me! God "knit me together in my mother's womb." As the psalmist went on to say, "Wonderful are thy works! Thou knowest me right well. . ." (v. 14).

There are other verses of this psalm and other parts of the Bible that present the image of a loving Creator who shapes and fashions us to fulfill a special purpose. Jeremiah, for example, was known by God before his birth and called to be a prophet. Here is how Jeremiah put it:

Now the word of the Lord came to me saying, "Before I formed you in the womb I knew you, and before you were born I consecrated you; I appointed you a prophet to the nations" (Jer. 1:5).

Based on Scripture, then, we have reason to believe that even before we were born, each of us was gifted by

God in certain ways and for certain purposes. If God is therefore the source of what Jung called our psychological predisposition to develop certain personality tendencies, then it becomes all the more important to discover what our personality gift is, because *that gift comes from God.*

Of all the spiritual gifts that can be given to us, the gift of one's personality is probably the most basic. Other gifts that we may have, such as the gift of teaching or service, will be expressed through our particular personality. If we are to use the gift of our personality fully, it is essential for us to know what that personality gift is.

Jung helped us by writing about the major types of personalities that he observed in people. Unfortunately, while Jung wrote about a variety of personality types, he offered no easy way for the average person to identify them. That task was taken up later by a mother and daughter team, Katharine Briggs and Isabel Briggs Myers. To make Jung's theory helpful for as many people as possible, the Myers-Briggs Type Indicator® (MBTI™) was developed. It has become one of the most commonly used psychological instruments in the United States, and is used in many other countries as well. The MBTI is frequently used by Christian churches and organizations.

The MBTI indicates the direction of an individual's preference for either Extraversion or Introversion, either Sensing or Intuition, either Thinking or Feeling, and either Judgment or Perception. Dr. Gordon Lawrence, a highly respected teacher and a past president of the Association for Psychological Type, has provided a way to start thinking about the personality patterns that people have.

There is no substitute for taking the Myers-Briggs Type Indicator. But to get a *beginning* idea about your own personality pattern, complete the following activity that Dr. Lawrence outlines in his book, *People Types and Tiger Stripes* (Center for Applications of Psychological Type, 1982). Don't think of this exercise as a "test." There are no "right" or "wrong" patterns, and no "bad" patterns. Since all these personality types come from God, each one is good, useful, and even necessary in order that God's purposes be fulfilled.

As you answer the questions, don't think about the way you have to act to please others at work, school, or elsewhere, and don't answer according to the way you sometimes *wish* you were or the way someone else would *like* you to be. Answer the questions according to what is true for you *when you are relaxed and there is no pressure to be anybody but yourself.* Think back over your life and the ways you have really preferred to be all along when you have had the chance to be "just you." You will be asked to decide which of two statements describes you better. Since both choices reflect different gifts from God, the question is, in which way has God gifted *you?*

Which pattern describes you better, E or I?

E	I
E likes action and variety	I likes quiet and time to consider things
E likes to do mental work by talking to people	I likes to do mental work privately before talking
E acts quickly, sometimes without much reflection	I may be slow to try something without understanding it
E likes to see how other people do a job, and to see results	I likes to understand the idea of a job and to work alone or with just a few people
E wants to know what other people expect of him or her	I wants to set his or her own standards

An E's interest turns mostly outward to the world of action, people, and things. An I's interest turns more often to the inner world of ideas and private things. Everyone turns outward to act and inward to reflect. You must do both, but you are more comfortable doing one or the other, just as right-handers are more comfortable with the right hand.

Circle the E or the I in the margin below to show which pattern seems to fit you better:

E I E stands for Extraversion, which means outward turning.
I stands for Introversion, which means inward turning.

Which pattern describes you better, S or N?

S	N
S pays most attention to experience as it is	N pays most attention to the meanings of facts and how they fit together
S likes to use eyes and ears and other senses to find out what's happening	N likes to use imagination to come up with new ways to do things, new possibilities
S dislikes new problems unless there are standard ways to solve them	N likes solving new problems, and dislikes doing the same thing over
S enjoys using skills already learned more than learning new ones	N likes using new skills more than practicing old ones
S is patient with details but impatient when the details get complicated	N is impatient with details but doesn't mind complicated situations

An S pays most attention to the facts that come from personal experience. An S can more easily see the details, while an N can more easily see the "big picture." An N pays most attention to meanings behind the facts.

S and N are two kinds of perception, that is, two ways of finding out or giving attention to experiences. S stands for Sensing and

What Kinds of Personality Gifts Are There?

N stands for Intuition. Everyone uses both their Sensing and their Intuition to find out things. You use both, but you rely on one more than the other.

S N   Circle the S or N in the margin to show which pattern seems to fit you better.

Which pattern describes you better, T or F?

T		**F**	
T	likes to decide things logically	F	likes to decide things with personal feelings and human values, even if they are not logical
T	wants to be treated with justice and fair play	F	likes praise, and likes to please people, even in unimportant things
T	may neglect and hurt other people's feelings without knowing it	F	is aware of other people's feelings
T	gives more attention to ideas or things than to human relationships	F	can predict how others will feel
T	doesn't need harmony	F	gets upset by arguments and conflicts; values harmony

A T makes decisions by examining data, staying objective and cool. A T stands for Thinking judgment. An F makes decisions by paying attention to personal values. F stands for Feeling judgment. You make T and F judgments every day, but you trust one kind of judgment more than the other.

T F   Circle the T or F in the margin to show which pattern seems to fit you better.

Which pattern describes you better, J or P?

J	P
J likes to have a plan, to have things settled and decided ahead	P likes to stay flexible and avoid fixed plans
J tries to make things come out the way they "ought to be"	P deals easily with unplanned and unexpected happenings
J likes to finish one project before starting another	P likes to start many projects but may have trouble finishing them all
J usually has mind made up	P usually is looking for new information
J may decide things too quickly	P may decide things too slowly
J wants to be right	P wants to miss nothing
J lives by standards and schedules that are not easily changed	P lives by making changes to deal with problems as they come up

J   P   Circle the J or P in the margin to show which pattern seems to fit you better. J stands for judgment and P stands for perception. J people show to others their thinking or feeling judgment more easily than they show their sensing and intuitive perception. The opposite is true for P people; they show their sensing or intuition rather than judgment in dealing with the world outside themselves.

Type comes from patterns

Now you can put together the four letters of the patterns that seem to describe you best. Draw a circle here around the same letters you circled in the margins above.

E I   S N   T F   J P

Now write your four letters here: ____ ____ ____ ____

The four letters together make up a whole pattern called a "type." It may be your type. There are 16 different "people types" as shown by the 16 combinations of the letters. Find the combination of four letters that may be yours.

ISTJ	ISFJ	INFJ	INTJ
ISTP	ISFP	INFP	INTP
ESTP	ESFP	ENFP	ENTP
ESTJ	ESFJ	ENFJ	ENTJ

If you have correctly identified your true personality gift from God, then the description under your four letters in the following Type Table should apply. Variations of this Type Table appear both on the MBTI Report Form and in *Introduction to Type* by Isabel Briggs Myers (Consulting Psychologists Press, 1976). *Introduction to Type* (Revised, 1987) also includes a more detailed, full-page description of each personality gift. *Introduction to Type* (ITT) is inexpensive and is available from Consulting Psychologists Press (P.O. Box 11636, Palo Alto, CA 94306) or the Center for Applications of Psychological Type (2720 N.W. 6th St., Gainesville, FL 32609; abbreviated as CAPT).

Characteristics frequently associated with each type

SENSING TYPES WITH THINKING (ST)   SENSING TYPES WITH FEELING (SF)

ISTJ	**ISFJ**
Serious, quiet, earn success by concentration and thoroughness. Practical, orderly, matter-of-fact, logical, realistic, and dependable. See to it that everything is well organized. Take responsibility. Make up their own minds as to what should be accomplished and work toward it steadily, regardless of protests or distractions. Live their outer life more with thinking, inner more with sensing.	Quiet, friendly, responsible, and conscientious. Work devotedly to meet their obligations. Lend stability to any project or group. Thorough, painstaking, accurate. Their interests are usually not technical. Can be patient with necessary details. Loyal, considerate, perceptive, concerned with how other people feel. Live their outer life more with feeling, inner more with sensing.
ISTP	**ISFP**
Cool onlookers, quiet, reserved, observing and analyzing life with detached curiosity and unexpected flashes of original humor. Usually interested in cause and effect, how and why mechanical things work, and in organizing facts using logical principles. Live their outer life more with sensing, inner more with thinking.	Retiring, quietly friendly, sensitive, modest about their abilities. Shun disagreements, do not force their opinions or values on others. Usually do not care to lead but are often loyal followers. May be rather relaxed about assignments or getting things done, because they enjoy the present moment and do not want to spoil it by undue haste or exertion. Live their outer life more with sensing, inner more with feeling.
ESTP	**ESFP**
Good at on-the-spot problem solving. Do not worry, enjoy whatever comes along. Tend to like mechanical things and sports, with friends on the side. May be a bit blunt or insensitve. Adaptable, tolerant, generally conservative in values. Dislike long explanations. Are best with real things that can be worked, handled, taken apart, or put together. Live their outer life more with sensing, inner more with thinking.	Outgoing, easygoing, accepting, friendly, enjoy everything and make things more fun for others by their enjoyment. Like sports and making things happen. Know what's going on and join in eagerly. Find remembering facts easier than mastering theories. Are best in situations that need sound common sense and practical ability with people as well as with things. Live their outer life more with sensing, inner more with feeling.
ESTJ	**ESFJ**
Practical, realistic, matter-of-fact, with a natural head for business or mechanics. Not interested in subjects they see no use for, but can apply themselves when necessary. Like to organize and run activities. May make good administrators, especially if they remember to consider other people's feelings and points of view. Live their outer life more with thinking, inner more with sensing.	Warmhearted, talkative, popular, conscientious, born cooperators, active committee members. Need harmony and may be good at creating it. Always doing something nice for someone. Work best with encouragement and praise. Main interest is in things that directly and visibly affect people's lives. Live their outer life more with feeling, inner more with sensing.

What Kinds of Personality Gifts Are There?

INTUITIVES WITH FEELING (NF)

INTUITIVES WITH THINKING (NT)

INFJ	INTJ
Succeed by perseverance, originality and desire to do whatever is needed or wanted. Put their best efforts into their work. Quietly forceful, conscientious, concerned for others. Respected for their firm principles. Likely to be honored and followed for their clear convictions as to how best to serve the common good. Live their outer life more with feeling, inner more with intuition.	Usually have original minds and great drive for their own ideas and purposes. In fields that appeal to them, they have a fine power to organize a job and carry it through with or without help. Skeptical, critical, independent, determined, sometimes stubborn. Must learn to yield less important points in order to win the most important. Live their outer life more with thinking, inner more with intuition.
INFP	**INTP**
Full of enthusiasms and loyalties, but seldom talk of these until they know you well. Care about learning, ideas, language, and independent projects of their own. Tend to undertake too much, then somehow get it done. Friendly, but often too absorbed in what they are doing to be sociable. Little concerned with possessions or physical surroundings. Live their outer life more with intuition, inner more with feeling.	Quiet and reserved. Especially enjoy theoretical or scientific pursuits. Like solving problems with logic and analysis. Usually interested mainly in ideas, with little liking for parties or small talk. Tend to have sharply defined interests. Need careers where some strong interest can be used and useful. Live their outer life more with intuition, inner more with thinking.
ENFP	**ENTP**
Warmly enthusiastic, high-spirited, ingenious, imaginative. Able to do almost anything that interests them. Quick with a solution for any difficulty and ready to help anyone with a problem. Often rely on their ability to improvise instead of preparing in advance. Can always find compelling reasons for whatever they want. Live their outer life more with intuition, inner more with feeling.	Quick, ingenious, good at many things. Stimulating company, alert and outspoken, may argue for fun on either side of a question. Resourceful in solving new and challenging problems, but may neglect routine assignments. Apt to turn to one new interest after another. Skillful in finding logical reasons for what they want. Live their outer life more with intuition, inner more with thinking.
ENFJ	**ENTJ**
Responsive and responsible. Generally feel real concern for what others think or want, and try to handle things with due regard for the other person's feelings. Can present a proposal or lead a group discussion with ease and tact. Sociable, popular, sympathetic. Responsive to praise and criticism. Live their outer life more with feeling, inner more with intuition.	Hearty, frank, decisive, leaders in activities. Usually good in anything that requires reasoning and intelligent talk, such as public speaking. Are well-informed and enjoy adding to their fund of knowledge. May sometimes appear more positive and confident than their experience in an area warrants. Live their outer life more with thinking, inner more with intuition.

Each type is different from the others in important ways. As you come to understand the type ideas better, you will see how type affects your life with your friends and family, at school, on the job, and in your congregation.

In addition to your own personality pattern, perhaps the questions you have just answered also give you an idea as to the preferences of some of your family and friends. An "idea" is all we can have about someone else for several reasons. First, Gordon Lawrence developed the questions only as a discussion starter. Since the questions were not created by research, you may not be able to rely on the results you get from them. Second, what we usually see in others is their *public* behavior, not their inner thoughts and feelings. People may not show in public what they really prefer. *Until a person has taken the Myers-Briggs Type Indicator and verified the results, we cannot draw any reliable conclusions about Type preference.*

Mike and Ellen: Gifted Differently

For purposes of illustration, we can think about the possible personality preferences of the couple we have met, Mike and Ellen. Mike is oriented outward toward the world of things and people. He appears to be what Jung called an extraverted personality (E), someone who picks up energy in interaction with people. Ellen, on the other hand, is not as action-oriented as Mike. She spends considerable time reflecting on her experiences and, like others who prefer introversion (I), she likes quiet time to think things through before she is ready to bring her ideas out into the open.

Mike and Ellen also have two different ways of looking at what is going on around them. The kind of work Mike does (and enjoys) requires that he pay close attention to specific facts and figures. For Ellen, this would take a great deal of energy, since she is less interested in such details. Rather than use her senses keenly as Mike does, Ellen takes a more intuitive approach to situations and problems. Mike observes closely, watching and listening, rarely letting a fact slip by. Ellen is more excited about using her present experience to imagine possibilities for the future. Rather than focusing on the facts, she tries to see what kind of meaningful patterns can be created out of the bits and pieces of everyday life. From the descriptions, we can see that Mike seems to be what the Myers-Briggs Indicator calls an Extraverted Sensing type (ES) and Ellen an Introverted Intuitive (IN).

Mike and Ellen also have different gifts when it comes to the ways they make decisions. Because Mike has a natural ability to think things through logically, analyzing the facts and remaining objective so as to be fair, he has the characteristics of a Thinking type (T). Ellen makes rational decisions too, but her rationale is different from Mike's. The crucial question for Ellen is whether or not the decisions she makes are sensitive to people's feelings and based on person-centered values. One of those central values is maintaining harmony in her relationships. Ellen will sometimes settle for a decision that may not be completely fair to her—if by doing so she can avoid interpersonal conflict. In contrast to Mike's thinking judgments (T), Ellen approaches decision making with Feeling (F). If we summarize what we have learned so far about Mike and Ellen, it appears that Mike prefers Extraversion, Sensing, and Thinking (EST), while Ellen prefers Introversion, Intuition, and Feeling (INF).

Finally, Mike is a person who likes a well-ordered, organized way of life. He is decisive, not always enjoying the decisions that must be made, but preferring to get the decision behind him so he can get on with life. This is what the MBTI calls a Judging type* (J). By way of contrast, Ellen tries to keep all of her options open as long as

---

*Judging, in MBTI language, does *not* mean judgmental. (See Chapter 3).

possible. In her teaching, she has an approach to the class in mind, but it does not bother her if the discussion takes an unplanned turn. She prefers to go with the flow, and she adapts well to the unexpected, as do most Perceptives (P).

From the perspective of the Myers-Briggs, a person like Ellen or Mike has a personality type which is the combination of the four preferences. We'll be looking at Ellen later, but in Mike's case, his personality seems to have the ESTJ type pattern. Now, notice that it is possible to place the four letters, ESTJ, in a variety of combinations, each of which says something true and important about Mike. For example, we can take the first two letters, ES, and speak of Mike as an Extraverted Sensing type. Or we can take the Sensing and Judging gifts and speak of Mike as an SJ. Or just looking at the Sensing and the Thinking makes it possible to think of Mike as an ST.

These two-letter combinations can be useful at times, as Isabel Briggs Myers has helped us see. On the basis of her research, type theory, and my own observations over the years, I want to look at four particularly important two-letter combinations: ST, SF, NF, and NT. My goal, however, is to provide a general way to think about people and situations, not a specific prescription for any individual person. God has created us much too marvelously to be understood fully by any simple psychological formula. However, you may find it helpful to have some general guidelines when trying to interpret what you observe in yourself and others, as long as you use those guidelines tentatively.

We will begin in the next chapter by looking at the ST combination we seem to have found in Mike. As an ST, Mike has a gift that all other ST's have, whether they are Extraverted or Introverted, Judging or Perceptive. Persons like Mike who have the ST combination (as in I*ST*J, I*ST*P, E*ST*P, or E*ST*J) can be said to have a natural tendency to develop the gift of practicality.

CHAPTER THREE

The Gift of Practicality: Living in the Here and Now

Mike would be quite happy being thought of as a practical person. If he were also called "realistic," he would accept it as a compliment. When others recognize our strengths, we feel affirmed. When others not only recognize but also let us know that they value our gifts, we feel appreciated.

Mike is appreciated at work. The "Office Manager of the Year" award he was given was based not only on a particularly good company record that year (with minimal absenteeism and high morale among his staff), but also on his having a record of consistent evaluations as a person of unusual management ability. Mike knows how to be firm when the situation calls for it, and yet those who work for him consider him to be as fair a manager as they have ever had.

Last year a conflict arose between two of Mike's staff members. Mike did not take sides, even though he had a natural liking for one of the employees more than the other. He patiently listened to the details both staff members gave him, weighed the evidence, sorted through the

33

alternatives, and announced his decision and how he had arrived at it. The compromise that he recommended showed respect for both parties. While Mike's concern was to be fair rather than to be swayed by either his own feelings or the feelings of others, he was glad to learn that his friend did not feel abandoned, and the other employee did not feel that others had teamed up against him.

The strengths of an ST

What are the special strengths of persons to whom God has given the gifts of Sensing and Thinking (ST)? Because of their ability to focus on the facts and to handle these facts in an impersonal, objective way, ST persons like Mike can handle technical tasks with ease. STs are attracted to vocations like business, production, construction, banking, law enforcement, and sometimes, as Mike was, administration because these jobs give them the opportunity to use their natural talents.

The Sensing gift makes it natural for Mike to pay attention to all the relevant details of a situation—which helped him deal realistically with the dispute between his staff members. Mike also relies on experience, and he learns through the accumulation of his experiences and the experiences of others. This serves him well when faced with a problem. He is able to recall important details of previous events and applies what he has learned from past experiences with remarkable sureness and confidence.

When Mike's Sensing is combined with sound Thinking judgment, Mike not only remembers his experiences, he organizes them in such a way as to enable him to see flaws in advance, thus keeping his company from making costly mistakes. Mike asks a lot of *Why?* questions. What he is looking for in events is a cause-and-effect relationship. If he can analyze a situation back to the source of the problem, Mike then feels confident that he can avoid similar problems in the future.

Those who work with Mike also appreciate his consistency. He is not likely to change his approach from day to day because experience has taught him that some ways of going about the job are more efficient and lead to better results. In other areas of life, also, Mike has some clear ideas about what works best. Unless new evidence causes him to question his judgments, the attitudes and beliefs Mike holds five years from now will probably be similar to those he holds now. There is a certain rock-like stability and security that Mike presents to others that comes out of the particular way he combines his gifts of Sensing and Thinking as an ESTJ.

There are a number of reasons why Mike uses his Sensing and Thinking gifts in the ways that he does. Because he is an Extravert, he is attracted to work that allows him to manage people. If he were an Introvert, he might prefer a vocation where he could work more independently and concentrate more on managing facts than on managing people. For example, accounting might be very appealing to an introverted ST, just as electrical or mechanical engineering might be.

Furthermore, the J at the end of Mike's personality type (EST*J*) means that he is a Judging type who likes organization and orderliness. He prefers to be on top of a situation—not necessarily controlling, but certainly in control of whatever he perceives to be his responsibility. If instead of being a Judging type he were a Perceptive (P), such as an EST*P* or an IST*P*, Mike might prefer a more flexible work environment where he could adapt to new circumstances as they arise. Vocations like marketing and mechanical work could have a particular attraction. However, Mike's work as an office manager in a marketing firm is very consistent with his gifts as an ESTJ.

There have not been any surveys of the general population that would tell us exactly how many people share Mike's preferences for ST. One of the best estimates, however, comes from Isabel Briggs Myers's sample of 9,320 eleventh and twelfth grade high school males and females reported in the MBTI *Manual*. In this 1957 study, approximately 41% of the high school males and 23% of the females were ST. Other research recorded at the data bank at the Center for Applications of Psychological Type suggests the percentage of ST males could be even higher. ST males who, like Mike, are also Extraverted and Judging (ESTJ) may make up as many as 17% or more of the males who graduate from high school. In Myers's study approximately 13% of the high school females were ESTJ.

These figures may not be representative of the entire population because Mrs. Myers did her research in suburban Philadelphia. Would she have had the same results in another part of Pennsylvania, or in another state? The CAPT data bank includes the MBTI results of all persons whose answer sheets have been computer processed by CAPT, but the lack of a stratified, random sample makes it hard to draw general conclusions.

Until more accurate figures are available, I think the Myers study gives us at least some idea of how personality type may be distributed in the general population. Keep in mind that your own area of the country or your subculture or denomination could be different in some way from a general population picture, even if a completely accurate picture of the general population were available. Although estimates must be used cautiously, I will use the Myers study to suggest how often the different personality types seem to appear in each of the personality patterns that you will meet in your church.

STs and the church

What contributions do Sensing Thinking persons make to the church? ST persons are able and willing to do almost anything they are asked to help with, but what really makes sense to them is to be given a task that makes some practical difference in the life of the congregation. For example, counting the offering, keeping the books, preparing and managing a budget, taking care of the church property, teaching neighborhood youth a useful trade or skill, or keeping supplies ordered for a community kitchen are some of the jobs that STs do with ease and satisfaction.

Not all STs are the same, of course. As mentioned earlier, one ST might have been the oldest of a family of six children and another ST might be an only child or the youngest of four. One might be a male and another a female. One might recently have gone through a health crisis and the other may never have been seriously ill. Any ST will have a personal family history and a particular life situation that will affect the way that individual experiences and uses the ST gift.

Even if it were possible for the personal histories and life situations of two STs to be identical, there may be other differences. Along with Sensing and Thinking, one of the STs could also be an Extravert (*E*ST) and the other an Introvert (*I*ST). Also, every ST prefers *either* order and organization (Judging) *or* adaptability and flexibility (Perceptive). If you put these various preferences together, there are four possible ST combinations: ESTJ, ESTP, ISTP, and ISTJ. Each type has something very important to offer a congregation. Let's look at some of the gifts each type brings.

ESTJ

Through Mike, we have already learned some things about what an ST who is Extraverted and Judging (ESTJ) might contribute to a congregation. For example, being asked to be on or to take charge of a task force could be very appealing. What people are likely to see in Mike is his Thinking ability to analyze situations and come to practical, logical conclusions. As a leader, an ESTJ will want to set realistic goals and will try to get the job done well and on schedule. An ESTJ like Mike will also want his or her work to have tangible results.

ESTP

Church members who prefer Extraversion, Sensing, Thinking, and *Perception* (ESTP; approximately 9% of the males and 4% of the females in Myers's high school study) will probably prefer to contribute to action-oriented projects that are problem-solving in nature. Because they are adaptable and open-minded, other people usually like ESTPs and are willing to follow their lead in finding new ways to tackle tough problems. An ESTP has a special ability to see the need of the moment and meet it with relative ease. Since ESTPs often enjoy physical activity, if the youth of the congregation need someone to head a softball team for the church league, an ESTP might be just the right person for the job.

ISTP

If Sensing, Thinking, Perceptive church members are *introverted* rather than extraverted (ISTP; about 6% of the male and 2% of the female students in Myers's study), then in their more quiet way they are probably interested in how and why things work. Their interest, however, isn't theoretical, but lies in practical application. Many ISTPs have technical or mechanical abilities, but not all prefer to work with their hands. An ISTP in the congregation might come up with a simplified way to keep the church accounts or a new way to invest the church's funds. The

ISTP may not want to·keep the records once these projects are initiated, as ISTPs usually prefer a more physically active role.

ISTJ

An IST who prefers *Judging* (ISTJ; about 9% of the male and 5% of the female students in Myers's study) may be just the person to keep the books. Extremely dependable, accurate, and thorough, ISTJs can be counted on to do whatever they commit themselves to do. An ISTJ is usually conservative, valuing what has worked well before and reluctant to make a change that is not really needed. They may have a strong interest in history and could be very helpful in putting together a history of the congregation. Recent research suggests there may be more ISTJ males and females than originally estimated.

Appreciating and supporting an ST

As you read some of the descriptions of the ST personality, perhaps you began to see yourself. Or maybe you saw your spouse, someone in your family, or a friend. Since approximately 33% of the general population may share the gifts of the ST, it would not be surprising if quite a few of those you know from home, work, or your congregation have these gifts. Of course, if we look at the "Type Table" on p. 28, we can see that the ST gifts are expressed in a variety of ways: ISTJ, ISTP, ESTP, and ESTJ (Mike's personality). At the top of page 40, the STs are highlighted on a Type Table of the 16 possible personality combinations.

Based on the earlier descriptions of the four ST personality types listed in the first column, see if you can identify at least one person gifted by God as an ST in each of your three main contexts for Christian living—at home,

ISTJ	ISFJ	INFJ	INTJ
ISTP	ISFP	INFP	INTP
E**ST**P	ESFP	ENFP	ENTP
E**ST**J	ESFJ	ENFJ	ENTJ

outside the home (school, work, community), and in the congregation. If you think you perceive the ST gifts in someone, write that person's name on the appropriate line on p. 41. *Be sure to write in pencil,* because you may change your mind later, or, if you talk with that person, he or she may help you realize that their actual gift from God is different from what you thought it was. Remember, unless a person takes a Myers-Briggs Type Indicator and, after a proper interpretation, agrees with the results, all we can really have is "an idea" about what any person's gifts actually are (including our own). We should remain open to the possibility of learning more. And even when we have correctly identified the personality type, that does not explain everything. *A person is more than what can be identified by any psychological instrument.* Those who *understand* the MBTI always make its limitations very clear.

In spite of these limitations, it can still be helpful for the improvement of relationships and for knowing how to be a good, supportive Christian friend if we can have at least "an idea" of how God has gifted someone with whom we live, work, or worship. In the space below, see if you can pencil in one or two names of people you believe may be gifted with ST. When you think about your congregation, don't forget to consider your pastor or other congregational leaders as possible STs.

After reading "The Strengths of an ST" and "STs and the Church";

Has God gifted someone in your family as an ST?

Circle one, if possible

_____   (ISTJ, ISTP, ESTP, ESTJ)

_____   (ISTJ, ISTP, ESTP, ESTJ)

Has God gifted someone at work/school/etc. as an ST?

Circle one, if possible

_____   (ISTJ, ISTP, ESTP, ESTJ)

_____   (ISTJ, ISTP, ESTP, ESTJ)

Has God gifted someone in your congregation as an ST?

Circle one, if possible

_____   (ISTJ, ISTP, ESTP, ESTJ)

_____   (ISTJ, ISTP, ESTP, ESTJ)

Now, with these persons in mind, let's think about how you might show your appreciation and support for those to whom God has given the gift of Sensing and Thinking (ST).

First, remember that the biblical way of looking at a person is as a *whole* person—a physical, thinking, feeling, relating person whose ultimate center is in God. If we are to appreciate and support those who are gifted as Sensing Thinking types, then we must understand their needs in each of these dimensions of life.

The *physical* dimension is important for Sensing persons. Those gifted with Sensing are usually more attuned to their bodies than are Intuitives. Sensing persons learn to rely on their senses to give them accurate information, and they are likely to be aware of any sign that their bodies are not in good shape. Because they enjoy the physical, Sensing persons often are interested in physical activities, including exercise and athletics. They are sensitive to hunger and thirst and are not apt to forget mealtimes. The Sensing person would like other Christians to understand his or her care of the body as an aspect of personal stewardship.

In the *mental* dimension, Sensing Thinking types are realistic, down-to-earth persons who think through problems in a logical, common-sense way. They need to be given as many relevant facts as possible, clearly and simply, if they are to do their best work. Their approach is unbiased and careful and they appreciate being praised for their accuracy and attention to detail when such praise is deserved.

An ST needs the most understanding and support in the *emotional* area. When Thinking is a person's gift, then the Feeling side of life tends to be less familiar and the Thinking type may be less confident when it comes to feelings. For instance, an ST spouse, child, or friend may not talk a lot about feelings. Being a Thinking type, an ST like Mike will probably talk more about what he is doing or thinking than he will about how he *feels* about what he is doing or thinking.

Mike may also neglect to ask Ellen about *her* feelings. This does not mean that Mike doesn't care about Ellen; it is just that his way of showing his care is by asking her what she thinks about things, or by doing things for her. He is less likely to initiate more intimate, feeling-oriented communication. If a Feeling type is married to or is close friends with a Thinking type, it will be important to understand that the Thinking person's neglect of the feeling area is not necessarily a lack of caring, but the result of having a different gift. With that awareness, the Feeling person will not be as likely to feel ignored or hurt. On the other hand, since other people's feelings are a fact to be taken into consideration when analyzing a situation, it is helpful if those feelings are objectively pointed out to those who prefer Thinking. Another time when Thinking types can use support is during those periods when they experience reversals or losses. Since their feelings may be less accessible to them, it can sometimes be helpful to invite them to talk about their experiences and then to ask them about their reactions to those events.

Socially it makes a lot of difference whether an ST is an Extravert or an Introvert. Extraverts tend to get their energy from being with other people and being involved in activities. Introverts are energized by inner resources and get drained by too much external involvement. The support that is needed will differ, since an Extraverted ST is a "hands-on" person who likes to be involved and who likes a lot of action, while an Introverted ST appreciates having time alone for uninterrupted reflection.

Spiritually an ST will be nurtured more in some ways than in others. While willing to sit patiently when another kind of sermon is preached, the sermons that make the most sense to an ST are grounded in real life and offer very realistic and practical applications. Worship services will appeal to an ST*J*, like Mike, if they are well-planned, orderly, and punctual. An ST*P* will respond better to a more spontaneous service, but, like the STJ, prefers a down-to-earth approach. STs like whatever happens at the service (songs, rites or rituals, activities) to have a clear connection with the Scriptures being read or the announced theme for the day—a logical connection that makes sense. Most importantly, they want to see a connection between Sunday's service and Monday's responsibilities.

In education classes, a Sensing Thinking person is a linear learner. That means that an ST will appreciate being led through a topic step-by-step. The ST will probably appreciate direct experience, lectures, and audiovisuals. How structured and organized the lesson needs to be will depend on whether the ST is a Judging or Perceptive type, but having some structure should be helpful in either case. To have a specific Scripture passage that supports what is being taught can be very helpful to some STs. The preferred learning environment, whether the ST enjoys working alone or in a group on a project, has to do with an ST's preference for Introversion or Extraversion. The Extraverted ST will in particular enjoy group competition and class reports.

Regarding pastoral care, persons gifted as STs want to feel valued not only as persons who have something to contribute, but just for being themselves. STs may not expect a great number of personal pastoral visits, but will appreciate being specifically asked for their opinion when important congregational decisions are made, particularly if those decisions affect the practical, day-to-day operation of the church. STs may need pastoral support if they are to grow in their appreciation for the global mission of the church, especially if there appears to be no direct connection between that mission and the ministry of the congregation. Once that connection is made, however, STs can be among the strongest supporters of mission efforts. Their focus on what is seen may limit their awareness of the value of the unseen and the place of the mystical in religious experience. However, STs will fully understand the need to embody religious values in concrete ways in the midst of the struggles of everyday life, and their willingness to serve will be an inspiration to many.

If your pastor appears to be an ST, then remember that most of what is true of other STs will be true of your pastor as well. Pastors, too, need your appreciation and support in the ways we have discussed. In addition, your pastor's personality will affect the way the pastoral role is carried out, and may in some ways even affect the shaping of that role. For example, an ST pastor whose Sensing and Thinking gifts are well-developed will be very reality-oriented and practical. If the ST preference is accompanied by a Judging (orderly and organized, *not* judgmental) orientation to life, then the pastor will be quite attentive to organizational matters in the congregation and will probably approach things in a structured way. An STP pastor will be equally realistic and practical, but will prefer a somewhat less organized approach to congregational life. Instead of order, the strength of an STP pastor is flexibility and adaptability and an appreciation for the excitement of life.

To further apply ST insights to an ST pastor, simply read over the description of the "Strengths of an ST" and "STs and the Church" and think about your pastor in relation to those descriptions. Then thank God for gifting your pastor in the way that God has! At the same time, in those areas of congregational life where there are needs that call for different gifts than your pastor has, these are the places where the gifts of congregational members will be especially needed.

One of the reasons I am especially drawn to the Myers-Briggs as it applies to the church is the way the MBTI points out how very much we Christians need each other. No one has *all* the gifts God gives. However, within the body of Christ God has given us all the gifts we need to be effective and faithful witnesses to God's love. If we can only appreciate this diversity of gifts as necessary for carrying out our Christian mission, then we will come closer to being the priesthood of all believers that the Bible calls us to be.

Sharing the ST gift

Not everyone is blessed with the gift of Sensing and Thinking, but everyone can share the gift. First, we can continue to appreciate, affirm, and support ST persons in our homes, schools, work, communities, and congregations. By doing so we will encourage our ST sisters and brothers to use their gifts.

As Isabel Briggs Myers has pointed out, much of the conflict people experience, and many of our feelings of being let down by others, are caused by our failure to recognize the gifts of people whose strengths are different from our own. That we have differing gifts is an undeniable message of the Bible. That God is the giver of those gifts is also clear. So the first way to share the gift of an ST is to give God thanks for it and affirm that individual in every way possible.

If you are not a Sensing Thinking type, two other ways to share the gift that STs have are: (1) to do your best to develop the ST gift in yourself, and (2) to ask those who have the gift to help you when you are doing something that requires ST skills. While you may not have Sensing and Thinking as your primary gift, you are certainly capable of acquiring and developing in yourself some of what comes naturally to an ST. As a matter of fact, it is very important that we learn to use each of the gifts when we are in a situation that calls for that gift. Whether or not we have the Thinking gift, there are times when we need to use that gift (such as when we need to balance our checkbook). Whether or not we have the Feeling gift, there are times when it is desirable to use that gift (for example, when someone needs our consolation).

There is, of course, a difference between having Sensing and Thinking as a *gift* and using ST as a *skill.* Gordon Lawrence says it is like a right-hander writing his or her name with the right hand, and then trying to write with the left. Try writing your first name, first with your dominant hand and then with your other hand. Using your nondominant hand is harder, feels awkward, takes more time, and requires a lot of concentration and energy. But it can be done and, in time, perhaps done quite well. You can acquire the skill—even though you will probably never be quite as comfortable with the skill as those who have the gift.

If we truly value the contribution that the Sensing person makes, we can begin to acquire skill in that gift by paying attention to the specifics in the here-and-now, gathering facts and data, and not jumping over relevant points in our Intuitive haste to see the "big picture." We can also temper our Feeling judgments with a careful, logical analysis of the information at our disposal. The best decisions are those that are made using both Sensing *and* Intuition, both Thinking *and* Feeling. Two of those are ours by gift, two we can only attain by hard work. If you are *not* gifted as an ST, then share the gift by practicing what you see come so naturally to those who are.

A second way to share the ST gift is to ask a Sensing Thinking person for help in situations where what needs to be done requires the ST gift. For example, I asked several ST persons to read this chapter and offer their suggestions. I benefited from their advice (and also from their proofreading ability). When I do statistical research, I find it very helpful to ask an ST to help me compile the data. By working side-by-side with people who have differing gifts, I have come to a greater appreciation of them as persons. I have also learned from them how to incorporate some of their gifts into my own life and work.

Learning to develop and incorporate the differing gifts of others is not only a caring, Christian thing to do, it is also an *essential* thing to do for your own development as a whole person in Christ. In early life, our task is to recognize and develop God's special gifts to us so that we can be sure to use our gift effectively and faithfully "to equip the saints for the work of ministry, for building up the body of Christ" (Eph. 4:12). As we mature, however, and especially around mid-life and later, a deeper and more complete personal integration results from our becoming more comfortable with those gifts that are the opposite of our own. Becoming all that we are capable of being involves learning to incorporate those opposite gifts more and more completely into our life. From this perspective, the efforts we make as Christians to appreciate and affirm those with gifts differing from our own can assist us in this personal growth toward wholeness. This is another beautiful example of how marvelously God has made us. "Give, and it will be given to you" (Luke 6:38). In the very process of responding to God's call to reach out to others, we are becoming more the people God calls us to be.

Now it is time to turn to those who have a different gift, one that is something like the ST but also *unlike* the ST in some very important ways. It is the gift of those who very naturally reach out to others and lift them up, *the gift of personal helpfulness.*

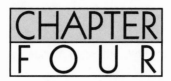

CHAPTER
FOUR

The Gift of
Personal Helpfulness:
Reaching Out and Lifting Up

When Mike and Ellen moved to Fairvue, Margie, their next-door neighbor, was very helpful. She seemed to know just the right time to come over with a tasty "treat," and just the right time to leave so as not to interfere with the moving-in process. It was the same blend of sensitivity and good judgment that made Margie one of the most popular nursing supervisors at the hospital. It also made her a most valuable addition to the church council.

Since Margie is probably typical of many active church members, let's take a look at persons like her who have the gift of personal helpfulness. It may help us to understand Margie's qualities if we compare her personality gifts with those we have already seen in Mike.

You may have noticed that Margie has some of the same personality characteristics that we found in Mike. That is because both of them are outgoing persons who use their Sensing to take in information and who prefer to live life in an organized and orderly way. In Myers-Briggs language, both Mike and Margie have the gifts of Extraversion, Sensing, and Judging (ES_J).

Where Mike and Margie differ is in how they prefer to make decisions. As we have seen, Mike combines his Sensing way of looking at things with a Thinking (logical and analytical) way of making decisions. This ST combination results in a very special gift, the gift of realism and practicality, and the ability to focus on the here-and-now.

Margie is also a present-oriented person, but she combines her Sensing way of perceiving with a different way of making decisions. She knows that it can be helpful to think through decisions logically and analytically, like Mike does, anticipating the consequences that will probably result from whatever action is taken today. However, when a really *significant* decision has to be made, Margie believes that logic cannot always be trusted. It may be the *logical* decision to make, but it may not *feel* right to her. Rather than rely on objective analysis, Margie's way of deciding is to base her decisions primarily on person-centered values. For her, cause and effect is spelled cause and *affect:* how will this particular decision affect people generally, and especially the important people in her life.

Jung said that to decide with Feeling (F) is every bit as rational as to decide with Thinking. It is just that the *rationale* is different. Mike makes the assumption that truth and fairness are fundamental to all choices, and his impersonal way of coming to a conclusion is not intended to be uncaring. On the contrary, Mike's *way* of caring is to make a decision as free as possible from personal bias.

In contrast with Mike, Margie's rationale is that, however valuable the head is in making decisions, the *heart* is what really matters. A decision can be made on the basis of impeccable logic, but such decisions may fail to appreciate the fact that life cannot be lived by analysis alone. Since preserving relationships is more important to Margie than being right, the only rational decision for her is one that shows warmth of heart and, insofar as possible, maintains harmony in her relationships.

The strengths of an SF

When Sensing and Feeling gifts are combined, persons like Margie are very much tuned into the people around them. SFs notice things about individuals. Margie can tell you whether a person is comfortable or uncomfortable and she can describe in remarkable detail the specifics that led her to a particular conclusion about someone. She is aware of herself as a physical person, so she tends to be observant of physical cues such as facial expressions.

While an SF like Margie is practical, her practicality is different from Mike's. Margie is not as interested in how things fit together as Mike has to be when he prepares his budget for next year. Margie is more interested in how *people* fit together and in the practical supports that people need in order to make that fit more harmonious and happy. If she has any interest in figures (like the number of milligrams in a dose of medication), it is primarily for the effect those numbers have on people.

With Extraversion, an SF like Margie will usually be among the first to reach out and offer help to someone in need. Since Margie is not only extraverted but also Judging (ESFJ), she is more likely to reach out in some *structured* context or role. For example, Margie reaches out in her position as a nurse, or as a member of the congregation's calling committee, or in the role of what she perceives to be a good neighbor or a good Christian.

People-oriented vocations are the ones most attractive to ESFJs (somewhere around 8% of the males and 20% of the females in Myers's study). An ESFJ might be drawn to nursing (especially to LPN, because of the practical work and greater personal contact) and medical secretary positions. They may also be interested in teaching or other work with young children. Religious education is also a popular choice. Many clergy are ESFJ. If ESFJs become salespersons, they would prefer to sell something tangible that is of direct benefit or pleasing to people. Making the home beautiful or helping others to dress well or to eat well (both amply and nutritionally) may be appealing.

SFs and the church

ESFJ

In the church, an ESFJ will probably be a willing volunteer for such things as a hospitality committee. Margie appreciates it if she can limit her commitment to a specific church event, such as a supper, reception, or tea, or a special gathering—something with a beginning and an end. Other attractive church activities include church school teaching, evangelism, and just about anything else that involves people working together. As an ESFJ, Margie likes group planning and committee work less for the task than for the social contact with other persons, and this is especially true if the group is not focused on a problem with immediate consequences for specific individuals. She dislikes abstract or theoretical discussions because she finds them boring if their direct relevance to everyday life is not clear. Margie is more interested in practical applications where she can see concrete results.

ISFJ

Many of these characteristics also apply to SFJs who are *introverted* (ISFJ; about 4% of males and 9% of females for Myers). While having similar interests, an introverted SFJ is not as likely as Margie to take the initiative unless he or she knows you well. Like the ESFJ, the ISFJ is very conscious of history and traditional values (home, country, and church). While *E*SFJs prefer an active approach to problem solving ("Let's get it done now!"), *I*SFJs need to think about it a little longer and prefer to keep things as they are for as long as possible. ISFJs are among the most willing and reliable of church volunteers, although they may need to be asked for their help, because initiation is less comfortable for Introverts.

ISFP

Some people have the gift of Introversion, Sensing, and Feeling but are *Perceptive* rather than Judging types (ISFP: about 5% of males and 6% of females for Myers). One difference between an ISFP and an ISFJ is that both are warm persons, but the ISFP keeps the feeling inside and does not show it as easily. ISFPs are very much aware of the sensory world and enjoy approaching the present in an unhurried manner. They may have a special love of nature and of animals. ISFPs are able to see immediate needs and are usually ready to do something to help out. They may really appreciate being asked to help because being asked overcomes their natural reticence to initiate. In drawing them into the work of the congregation, it may be helpful to remember that ISFPs are often better able to express their caring with deeds than with words. They may prefer to let the work of their hands speak for them. An ISFP will probably keep personal feelings and values inside unless those feelings or values are threatened. Then the ISFP will speak out. It is their core, inner values that provide direction for their lives.

ESFP

With *extraversion*, an SFP may be an excellent problem solver. ESFPs (approximately 7% of males and 12% of females for Myers) are keen observers of the human scene. Because of their winning way with other people, their perceptions are valued and their suggestions have a good chance of being followed. They like action and are often found in fields such as transportation and sales, or in up-front positions where they have people contact. ESFPs notice what goes on around them. Given the choice of experiencing life or reading about life, ESFPs will usually prefer firsthand experience. Consequently, the "school of life" may have more appeal for them than a college education. They believe that life is to be lived fully and freely, and is to be enjoyed. And they are enjoyable to be with. Among other things, an ESFP could make an excellent youth group advisor and an enthusiastic teacher for young people. ESFP's response and performance may actually be enhanced if they are asked to do something for a short time, or in rotation with others. ESFPs tend not to like having jobs hanging over their heads.

Appreciating and supporting an SF

You may have discovered yourself among those gifted as an SF. If not, perhaps you thought of someone else whom you know very well. Approximately 35% of the general population may share the gifts of the SF, so probably a goodly number of your friends and acquaintances are Sensing Feeling types. Now is the time to do what we did in the last chapter. Look at the Type Table at the top of page 55, which reminds you that the SF gift is expressed in the variety of ways we have just discussed—ISFJ, ISFP, ESFP, ESFJ.

Based on the descriptions of the four SF personality types in the second column of this Type Table, see if you can identify at least one person you believe God has gifted as an SF—at home, outside the home (school, work, or

ISTJ	**IS**FJ	INFJ	INTJ
ISTP	**IS**FP	INFP	INTP
ESTP	**ESF**P	ENFP	ENTP
ESTJ	**ESF**J	ENFJ	ENTJ

community), and in the congregation. Pencil the names into the spaces below, as you did for the STs. After reading "The Strengths of an SF" and "SFs and the Church":

Has God gifted someone in your family as an SF?
       Circle one, if possible
_____ (ISFJ, ISFP, ESFP, ESFJ)
_____ (ISFJ, ISFP, ESFP, ESFJ)

Has God gifted someone at work/school/etc. as an SF?
       Circle one, if possible
_____ (ISFJ, ISFP, ESFP, ESFJ)
_____ (ISFJ, ISFP, ESFP, ESFJ)

Has God gifted someone in your congregation as an SF?
       Circle one, if possible
_____ (ISFJ, ISFP, ESFP, ESFJ)
_____ (ISFJ, ISFP, ESFP, ESFJ)

Keeping these persons in mind, let's turn now to how you might show your appreciation and support for those to whom God has given the gift of Sensing and Feeling (SF).

If we take a "whole person" approach to appreciating and supporting SFs, we will see some similarities between SF and ST. This is because both have the gift of Sensing. Sensing persons usually place more of an emphasis on the *physical* and material than Intuitives do. It is a misperception to assume that this Sensing emphasis is "materialistic." Sensing persons are gifted with an appreciation of the tangible. They like to see, to hear, to taste, to smell, and to touch. They have the gift of present enjoyment. It is supportive to express thanks for what the Sensing person does by giving a tangible token of appreciation. Depending on gender and personal preferences, a flower, fruit, a gift for the house, a cross, or a pin to wear are examples of such recognition. Remembrances are particularly important for an SF, because they reinforce the value of the relationship.

Mentally, also, an SF and an ST have similarities. Both are linear learners, which means they prefer a certain approach to education. They like ideas and material presented in such a way that the learner can start at a clear beginning point and then proceed step-by-step toward the conclusion. Both STs and SFs like direct experiences and audiovisuals, which makes learning much more of a sensory experience. However, a Thinking person's more analytical bent makes a lecture more helpful to an ST than to an SF. An extraverted SF like Margie prefers a harmonious learning environment where there is a personal relationship with the teacher and lots of interaction with others in the group. She also prefers to put energy into working through problems only when she believes that specific, individual persons will benefit from that effort. Thinking for the sake of thinking, or debate for the sake of debate, seems to Margie like a waste of time. If in a discussion there are definite (but unclear) implications for the welfare of particular people, it can be helpful to point these implications out to an SF.

Emotionally, an SF is usually comfortable with feelings and relies on those feelings for making important decisions and choices. We can count on a person like Margie to have feelings for other people and to have a strong desire to help when help is needed. Because Margie and other SFs are likely to go out of their way to be helpful, other Christians need to be supportive of SFs in a special way. Of all the people in the congregation, those with SF gifts will probably be among the first to respond to a request for help and to keep on responding as long as the need exists. Consequently, in the church an SF is a prime candidate for burnout. SFs tend to be called upon too much and for too long. Others can be supportive by periodically checking with them on how they are doing and whether they might be in need of relief. The same thing can be true in a marital relationship or close friendship. SFs are likely to go to great lengths to keep their relationships harmonious and happy, sometimes to the point that they begin to feel hurt and let down when they do not feel equal investment from their partners. It is helpful to give an SF "permission" not to give beyond what he or she can give freely.

Socially, a great deal depends on whether or not an SF is an Extravert or an Introvert (as was true of STs as well). However, there is one difference between STs and the SFs in this regard. Because of their Feeling, an SF is people-oriented and will gravitate toward people. This interest may look like extraversion even if the SF is naturally introverted. However, the *I*SF is likely to tire more quickly in social situations than an *E*SF like Margie. An ISF therefore needs to be sure to build in some private time when there are heavy social demands. An Introverted SF is also apt to find small groups or one-on-one contact more rewarding than spending a lot of time in larger gatherings.

Spiritually, an SF is going to understand the Christian faith in terms of personal relationship. God the Father, a personal Savior, the church as family—these are vital ways to "enflesh" the faith for most SFs. As is true for STs, proclamation needs to be down-to-earth and practical. Margie, for example, likes her pastor to tell stories that make sense in terms of everyday living, particularly if they are told in a simple and straightforward manner and have the feel of being true or true-to-life. She appreciates receiving guidance on how to live a faithful life, and it is even more helpful if the guidance is somewhat detailed and each desirable step pointed out. An SF will appreciate this same approach in Sunday school and other educational settings.

In worship, an SF is responsive to an appeal to the senses. When Margie goes to church, she usually picks right up on changes or accents in light, color, or sound. She enjoys colorful liturgical paraments or other touches that make the worship service seem special. Margie also likes to sing the old, familiar hymns that tell of God's love and relationship with us, and she believes that hymns and music are missing something unless they are emotionally moving.

Tradition is important to an SF, especially if tradition is linked to a significant historical person. However, a part of the tradition that is particularly important to persons who share Margie's gifts is the way the church is to care for those less able to help themselves. Therefore, if there are children or elderly or handicapped persons present at worship, an SF will want to see the presence of those people affirmed. While very quick to pick up the presence of needy persons in the immediate environment, an SF like Margie sometimes will be slower to respond to the more general causes of the church. In order to make the wider mission of the church more relevant, it may be helpful to inform an SF like Margie about the needs of a specific mission effort and the problems of some individual missionaries as a way of concretizing the commitment of the church.

If your pastor appears to be an SF, then reread "The Strengths of an SF" and "SFs and the Church" with your pastor in mind, since most of what applies to other SFs will apply to your pastor as well. Along with those general insights, you might want to consider that it will be very important for your pastor to feel the appreciation of the congregation. The pastor will probably go to great lengths to see that the needs of other people are met. Recognizing that effort from time to time and making sure that the pastor has sufficient help are two ways to show appreciation. Another way to affirm an SF pastor is to do your best to help the congregation be a happy and harmonious place for people. An SF pastor will be very happy if people in the congregation genuinely care for one another.

Sharing the SF gift

It is probably accurate to say that the church as most of us know it would be dramatically different without the SF gifts of persons like Margie. The friendly greeting, the warm smile, and the helping hand are all offered quite naturally by an SF. The focus on the individual person, the advocacy of specific and tangible help in concrete situations, and the willingness to volunteer to carry such programs out are related gifts—not exclusive to SFs, but very characteristic of them.

Not everyone has the SF gift. If you are an ST like Mike, it will be important that you give very conscious attention to person-centered values when you make decisions. Since Feeling is often one of the lesser developed capacities of Thinking types, an ST may underestimate how much energy it may take to concentrate on people's feelings and on what works to create harmony in family or group situations. If done superficially by an ST, an emphasis on feelings lacks a sense of authenticity. However, an ST who takes the extra time to check out how people are feeling about the way the task, a job, or a decision is being accomplished will find that effort well-rewarded by the appreciation of family, friends, and coworkers.

While it takes effort for an ST to share the gift of an SF, an *Intuitive* Thinker (NT) must work even harder. If you are an NT, you have exactly the opposite preferences of the SF—Intuition instead of Sensing, and Thinking instead of Feeling. A good beginning point for an NT is genuinely to appreciate the SF's gift for creating warmth and harmony in specific life situations. The more globally-oriented and abstract-thinking NT may be tempted to depreciate the significance of the SF's concentration on one-to-one or local group relationships. Perhaps seeing this SF form of ministry as a potential springboard to wider mission would help NTs to see the value of developing even more of those skills themselves.

NFs like Ellen have an easier time sharing the gift of an SF because they have the gift of Feeling in common. Since both use person-centered values in their decision making, there is some sense in which we might say that SFs and NFs "speak the same language." However, to share the special gift of the SF, an NF will need to focus more on specific persons and interpersonal relationships in the present rather than quickly taking an intuitive leap ahead into the more general perception of future possibilities.

Other differences between the SF and the NF gift will become apparent as we turn now to those like Ellen who use their gift of *possibilities for people* as a way of keeping hope alive.

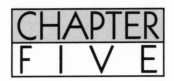

CHAPTER
FIVE

The Gift of
Possibilities for People:
Keeping Hope Alive

There could hardly have been a better evangelist than Margie was during Ellen's move to Fairvue. Ellen responds very well to people like Margie. She likes the personal touch. Ellen also shares Margie's understanding of the church as a friendly, helping community.

The common link between Ellen and Margie is their reliance on Feeling. Ellen has always been a sensitive person. Growing up, she was aware of the feelings of others, able to pick up the smallest cues of discomfort or pain in her family or among her playmates. Something inside her just naturally responded to those who were hurting, and that "something" called her to do whatever she could to help.

As Ellen learned more about Jesus in Sunday school, it was Jesus' healing ministry that especially attracted her. She could imagine Jesus looking compassionately at the crowds, noticing the people with particular needs, speaking to them, reaching his hands out to touch them, and restoring them to health and wholeness. As she grew, she was also drawn to Jesus' teachings. She began to see how they offered a way in which people could avoid having to hurt so much in the first place. Ellen began to think that maybe her place in life would be as a teacher. She started observing her teachers more closely so she could be like them.

One influential teacher in Ellen's life was her pastor. He had a special talent for putting into practice what he preached and taught about religion. He made an effort to spend time with the young people in the congregation so they could get to know him as a person. Ellen was impressed not only by her pastor's concern to gather food and clothing for poor families in the community, but even more by the fact that he personally delivered those gifts. She came to think of the church as God's way of carrying on Jesus' person-centered ministry in today's world. Ellen imagined what it would like to be a pastor, and the thought appealed to her. She felt it was unfortunate that her denomination did not permit the ordination of women.

Ellen's early idealism never left her, but it was gradually tempered by the realization that, despite good intentions, people do hurt each other. As much as she disliked seeing it happen, conflicts and alienation seemed to affect everyone sooner or later. Ellen decided that along with doing her best to help prevent such estrangements between people, she also wanted her life to give witness to the Christian message of reconciliation. As early as high school she became known as a person people could confide in. When she was told about a difficulty in a relationship, Ellen not only listened to what was said, but also tried to think of ways that the broken relationship might be restored. She never gave up. As far as she was concerned, there was always hope as long as two people were willing to talk.

After high school, Ellen entered college. She enjoyed reading and considered a number of different majors, including history, the arts, and literature. Anthropology attracted her, but there was no degree program in that area at the community college she attended. She decided to study for a degree in education and take as many anthropology, sociology, and psychology courses as she could.

Ellen met Mike in college. She realized that their personalities were very different, but that was partly what interested her. Ellen saw some real possibilities in working with Mike as a study partner. Eventually both she and Mike began to think that they could also make a good team as life partners. They complemented each other—the one able to do quite easily what the other struggled with. Upon graduation, Mike took an office job with the marketing firm where he continues to work. Ellen began teaching, stopped for a while when Andy was born, and then taught again until they moved to Fairvue.

When Mike and Ellen joined the church in Fairvue, it was not long before Ellen's obvious interest and ability in education prompted someone to ask her to be a substitute teacher for the adult class. Eventually, the class became her responsibility. One of the things that she did differently from any other teacher of that class was to add a personal touch, making a home visit to each of the members to learn more about them and to see if they had any special topics they might like the class to pursue. Above all, Ellen was concerned to encourage the class to focus on significant issues that had personal relevance.

The strengths of an NF

Throughout her story, we can see signs that Ellen has the gift of the Intuitive Feeler (NF). Of course, we already know through Margie some of the strengths of those who have the gift of Feeling. Their person-centered and relationship-oriented values provide the socio-emotional support that makes it possible for congregations and other social groups to live together in harmony.

In Margie, we saw how Feeling combined with Sensing (SF) results in the gift of personal helpfulness. When a Feeling person's way of perceiving is not Sensing but Intuition, what an Intuitive Feeling (NF) person like Ellen brings to her family, workplace, and congregation is the gift of being able to see possibilities. Because NF is a Feeling type, the possibilities that Ellen or any NF sees are primarily *possibilities for people.*

There are relatively few persons gifted with the combination of Intuition and Feeling, perhaps only about 14% of males (some indications are that there may be even fewer) and 20% of females (Myers). NFs tend to be enthusiastic and insightful persons who are good communicators. An NF gifted with Introversion (*I*NF) is often a good writer, and an Extraverted NF (*E*NF) is frequently a persuasive public speaker. In addition to the communication fields, NFs generally are attracted to such vocations as counseling, the social sciences, and the ministry.

Unless something happens during the growing up process that darkens his or her vision, an NF is usually quite idealistic. Sensing persons may question the practicality of some of the possibilities an NF perceives, which is a good reason for an NF to have some trusted Sensing friends who can help identify what it would take to translate a vision into reality. However, if there were no perception of the possibility in the first place, many opportunities would be lost. An NF has a special capacity to see what might be able to be done—with and by and for people.

NFs and the church

Ellen is a good example of the gifts an NF can bring to the church. Her enthusiasm and insight and her ability to draw people into a discussion make her an ideal leader for the congregation's adult study group. Her idealism keeps her constantly searching for ways in which the church can be more faithful in mission and more effective in ministry. She would enjoy being a member of a long-range planning committee that would project the possible directions the congregation could take over the next five or ten years. Ellen would be especially sensitive to the way in which the congregation responded to the personal needs of its members, but she would be equally concerned if the congregation were not responding to the needs of others in the community or in the world.

INFP

Because Ellen is also gifted as an Introvert and a Perceptive (INFP: about 3% of males and 4% of females in Myers' high school study), she might be more interested in developing new ideas for the congregation's ministry than in being the one who implements them. She would also want to see a good deal of flexibility built into any projected program so that there could be a change in direction if the circumstances changed. An INFP may not choose to be a teacher in the church, as Ellen did, but the church's educational program would probably be one of the priorities for an INFP in any case. While he or she is often quiet and reserved, an INFP's strength comes from deeply held core convictions that he or she may not often talk about. An INFP may be a leader in bringing about change in the direction of those underlying values.

ENFP

With *Extraversion* (ENFP: approximately 6% of males and 9% of females, Myers), an NFP may well be among the more charismatic persons in a congregation. ENFPs have a very strong intuitive gift that enables them to see opportunities that other people may overlook, and they are often able to provide the impetus for getting the congregation to do something about those opportunities. While they may need to be careful not to get too many balls in the air at the same time, they are at their best when, as a pastor or as a layperson, they are helping other people realize their potential for growth.

ENFJ

An Extraverted NF with a *Judging* gift (ENFJ: about 3% of males and 4% of females, Myers) shows Feeling to others in warm and friendly ways. The concern for harmony shared by all NFs is usually one of their most obvious personality characteristics. ENFJs are often among the more loyal and conscientious followers of persons they admire or causes they undertake. They both affirm others and appreciate affirmation from others. In a parish program, an ENFJ might make a fine Christian educator or leader of one of the congregation's programs. An ENFJ may be very much drawn to ordained or lay professional ministry.

INFJ

When those gifted with NFJ are *Introverted* (INFJ: about 2% of males and 2% of females in Myer's high school research), their Feeling is what others are more likely to see, but their inner Intuitive gift is dominant. Their intuition may help them perceive some very creative possibilities in complex situations. As Introverts, they may not take the initiative in sharing these perceptions. One way to help them make a real contribution to the church is to invite and welcome their insights. As with the other NFs, an INFJ is attracted to such fields as teaching, preaching, counseling, and the social sciences.

Appreciating and supporting an NF

Perhaps you have the NF gift. If not, maybe you have a family member or friend whom God has gifted with Intuition and Feeling. Available research suggests that there are fewer NFs in the general population than either ST or SF. Only about 17% of the people seem to have NF gifts. Perhaps my description of the various ways in which the NF gift is expressed reminded you of someone you know. An NF, of course, could be either INFJ, INFP, ENFP, or ENFJ.

ISTJ	ISFJ	**INF**J	INTJ
ISTP	ISFP	**INF**P	INTP
ESTP	ESFP	**ENF**P	ENTP
ESTJ	ESFJ	**ENF**J	ENTJ

On the basis of your reading of "The Strengths of an NF" and "NFs and the Church":

Has God gifted someone in your family as an NF? If so, pencil in their names:

Circle one, if possible

_____ (INFJ, INFP, ENFP, ENFJ)

_____ (INFJ, INFP, ENFP, ENFJ)

Has God gifted someone at work/school/etc. as an NF?

Circle one, if possible

_____ (INFJ, INFP, ENFP, ENFJ)

_____ (INFJ, INFP, ENFP, ENFJ)

Has God gifted someone in your congregation as an NF?
Circle one, if possible
_____ (INFJ, INFP, ENFP, ENFJ)
_____ (INFJ, INFP, ENFP, ENFJ)

Each of these persons is special and needs your appreciation and support. However, what is *experienced* by an NF as appreciative and supportive will be different in some ways from what those with ST, SF, or NT gifts consider supportive. How can you let Christian brothers and sisters who have the gifts of Intuition and Feeling know that you are with them? Once again, the whole person model will help guide us in knowing where the support is most needed.

An NF is more likely than the Sensing types to neglect the *physical* dimension of life and to pay insufficient attention to both physical and material needs. (This is particularly true of Introverted NFs, although some report that ENFPs are also likely to miss bodily cues.) Idealistic and future-oriented, an NF like Ellen often overlooks the physical requirements of the present. Ellen appreciates her Sensing friends who help her understand that she will have a better chance of realizing her goals if she does two things: take care of herself, and check out the practicalities of the goals she envisions. NFs need to remember to take some time for self-care because they throw themselves wholeheartedly into whatever it takes to realize their dreams. Those with such consuming passions can overlook obvious physical needs such as regular meals. Second, Sensing friends can encourage an NF to consider exactly what it will take to make the NF dream come true.

This need to underscore the practical is, of course, also a factor in the *mental* dimension. Intellectually, an NF is a global thinker who prefers to look at the "big picture." An ever-present possibility is that, in their desire to see how everything fits together, Intuitives may overlook essential Sensing facts without which it will be much more difficult to put their ideas into practice. It is supportive to point out relevant details to NFs, as long as it is done in a way that does not shoot down the ideas they are working on. It is also helpful to keep in mind that NFs might take the criticism of their ideas more personally than was intended. Ellen finds that the most constructive critique is one that takes her feelings into account.

An NF is usually at home with *feelings.* INFPs and ENFPs keep their feelings more on the inside, but the feeling side of life is vitally important to Ellen and all others who share the NF gift. Warm and friendly relationships are highly desired. An NF also has as a primary concern the maintenance of values that respect the needs of people. Most NFs will willingly spend a great deal of time and put a lot of emotional investment into helping the church become a place where people feel at home. NFs may need some support so they do not overextend themselves too far. Since it is difficult for NFs to say no when someone needs help, NFs share the SF's potential for overcommitment.

The Feeling gift will make it likely that an NF will be a socially sensitive person, whether Introverted or Extraverted. The difference is that the Introverted Feeling person may tire more quickly in an extraverted environment. Those pastors and laypersons who find social activity pleasant but draining need to be sure to set aside regular periods for quiet reflection if they want to avoid burnout. It is always important to remember that every gift has its strengths and its limitations.

NFs are among the most responsive to the idea of a *spiritual* quest, which may account for the high percentage of NFs in the clergy (in one report of 534 clergy, 55% were NF). NFs' idealism, enthusiasm, and people-orientation make them responsive to sermons that, through the personal sharing of the preacher, sketch out possibilities for people and present the challenges that Christians face in a complex world. I used the word *sketch* deliberately. NFs have a special love for the symbolic and metaphorical and do not need to have ideas spelled out in great detail. Their Intuitive gift enables them to fill in the blanks, and most NFs like a little room for imagination.

In worship, an NF will probably prefer an aesthetically pleasing service, with music appropriate to the mood. How much order and structure is desired will depend on whether an NF is a Judging or Perceptive person. They will tend to see Scripture, baptism, and the Lord's Supper as ways to underscore the relationship between God and the Christian community. Educationally, NFs will respond best to trusted teachers with whom they feel they have a personal relationship. They like to have a theory or general idea presented to them before considering applications, and if the theory is presented well enough they may prefer to make their own most relevant applications. NFs like open-ended instruction, where the beginning of an idea is given and then opened up for discussion.

If your pastor appears to be an NF, take another look at the sections on NF strengths and interests, then think of how that information might be helpful in understanding and relating to your pastor. The role of pastor, as understood by most church members, includes making appropriate use of the NF gift of recognizing possibilities for people and keeping hope alive. However, an NF pastor may need considerable support, especially from Sensing parishioners, to translate the NF vision into practical programs. Once again, however, it is well not to be too quick to point out the impracticality of an idea. An NF pastor will most appreciate those who recognize the value of an idea and who do their best to explore ways to make it work. Sometimes an NF pastor will have more ideas than resources to put those ideas into practice. Helping to point out realistic limits, coupled with an obvious willingness to work on implementing one or two promising programs, can come through as very supportive.

An NF pastor may be bothered by criticism. While you may only be criticizing the idea and not the person, an Intuitive Feeling pastor may take the criticism more personally than you intend. If an NF pastor feels well-regarded and loved by the person offering the critique, then it can be heard and handled much better. Consequently, any pastoral relations committee needs to be composed of individuals who are sensitive to an NF's need for warm, interpersonal relationships. With such emotional support, NF pastors will be at their best and their gifts will bring many blessings to their congregations.

Sharing the NF gift

As we have seen, one of the primary gifts of a NF is the ability to perceive possibilities. When people do not see any possibility in their situation, they are likely to feel helpless and eventually hopeless. An NF's capacity to see alternatives and choices enables him or her to bring a spirit of hopefulness into many situations. Being people-oriented, an NF has a natural empathy for those who are hurting or who feel boxed-in. While on a feeling level identifying with those having a problem, an NF also brings into the situation an Intuitive gift for recognizing the available options. When we begin to see that we have alternatives and that we are not alone, most of us renew our sense of possibility and hope.

As is true for any of the other gifts, to share the gift of an NF it is first desirable to appreciate and affirm that gift when you discover it in others. When NF people like Ellen feel affirmed, they are more likely to contribute what they have to offer in whatever situation they are in or whatever discussion they are having. Simply thinking along with an NF, trying to see things the way an NF perceives them, can contribute an awareness that there may be multiple ways to go about solving any given problem. An NF is also able to point out the possible emotional impact of each of the possible alternatives. Letting NFs like Ellen know that their gift is valued is the first way to share that gift.

An equally important goal for personal growth is to see if any of what comes naturally to people like Ellen can be cultivated within yourself. The first step is to say to yourself that, as impossible as it seems, there are always alternatives in any situation you are facing. A Christian NF knows that these possibilities do not come from the power of positive Intuitive thinking, but from Christ, who is with us in the midst of our life situations. With Christ present and caring in our lives, no situation is hopeless and every challenging situation presents us with an opportunity.

Once a person has accepted that there are alternatives, the next step is to consider what those alternatives might be. In some situations, perhaps the only alternative we can think of is whether we will face adversity with despair or with faith. But those are still alternatives that can make all the difference in the world in how we think and feel about ourselves and how we relate to others. To share the gift of an NF is to practice "never saying never," for the gift of an NF is to witness to the fact that with God all things are possible.

The gift of seeing possibilities is, of course, not restricted to NFs. We shall now look at another group of persons who have a sense of the possible, but who use it in a very different way: Intuitive Thinkers (NT). Persons gifted with NT have a particular passion for looking ahead and allowing what they "see" in the future to guide the present.

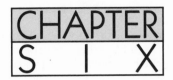

CHAPTER SIX

The Gift of Looking Ahead: Letting the Future Guide the Present

Ellen remembers well the first time she and Mike met their pastor. The first Sunday after they had moved to Fairvue, their already good neighbor, Margie, asked them to come over for a cookout to get away from all the unpacking, if only for a little while. They were told to come as they were, and they did.

Mike had taken over the grill while Margie was in the house looking for some homemade relishes. The hot dogs and hamburgers were just about ready when someone called Margie's name over the backyard fence. It was Margie's pastor, but Mike and Ellen didn't realize it right away because everybody was dressed casually and, with Margie away, there were no formal introductions. Margie had learned that her pastor was going to be home alone that Sunday and, in her friendly way, she mentioned on her way out of church that she was going to have a cookout and there was plenty of food.

The "newcomer" to Margie's cookout was outgoing, inquisitive, and helpful. Until Margie reappeared, the conversation was centered on Mike and Ellen, how they had happened to come to Fairvue, what kind of work they did, and some tips for finding their way around town and getting Andy enrolled in school. During what appeared to be small talk, the pastor was actually getting some idea of what kind of church programs and services would be attractive to this new couple. By the time the questions went the other direction, both Mike and Ellen were feeling comfortable with Margie's "unexpected" guest. Still, it was a bit of shock when Margie reappeared, relishes in hand, and said, "Oh, you've met my pastor!"

Since Mike had been on the church board in his former community and Ellen had been a Sunday school teacher, they were interested in learning more about the pastor and the church. What they discovered was that Pastor Lynn had quite an interesting history. Educated at one of the major seminaries in the country, there was, right after graduation, an opportunity to participate in a foreign exchange program. That experience had sensitized the pastor even more to the challenge of cross-cultural ministry and the need for the church to have a global perspective. Ellen was very pleased to learn about these experiences because she was hoping to find a church in Fairvue that looked beyond itself.

The thing that impressed Mike was that, while making mission a priority, Pastor Lynn did not in any way neglect the local ministry. And the pastor was very community conscious. It didn't all come out right away, but in time Mike and Ellen learned that in addition to being the chaplain for the Chamber of Commerce, Pastor Lynn also served on the city planning council.

Three months before, the pastor had learned at a planning council meeting that the neighborhood in which the congregation was located was going to feel the impact of a new industrial park. Housing contractors were already exploring the possibility of tearing down single-family dwelling homes and building an apartment complex just down the street from the church. And some of the businesses coming into the industrial park would be bringing employees in from other towns. One firm that was slated to move in was owned by a coalition of minority entrepreneurs.

Pastor Lynn was not at all disturbed by these developments, even though they might require a substantial shift in the way the congregation ministered to the community. In fact, the pastor thrived on managing change. Any change represented a challenge and every problem an opportunity. After careful analysis of the situation and appropriate consultation with community leaders, Pastor Lynn became convinced that the congregation would be able to let these developments guide their present programming. Above all, the pastor wanted to be sure the congregation would be able to provide a ministry to the changing neighborhood that would be competent and forward-looking.

The strengths of an NT

Pastor Lynn's ability to face the coming changes not only with equanimity, but with anticipation, is one of the strengths of the person gifted with Intuition and Thinking (NT). Others share the sense of possibility (particularly the NF), but an NT like Margie's pastor has an additional natural ability to logically analyze a situation, see the continuity between past, present, and future, and come up with a strategy that has a good chance of being effective.

One of the reasons Mike was impressed by Pastor Lynn is that Mike shares one of the pastor's strengths, the gift of Thinking. Mike was impressed both with Pastor Lynn's ability to make a careful analysis of the impending changes and continue that analysis to the point of thinking about the kind of practical programs that would be needed to implement a change strategy. Ellen was drawn to Pastor

Lynn because she recognized that the pastor had an Intuitive mind like hers. She shared with Pastor Lynn the larger concern about how the church can offer its witness in the world. But although Mike has the Thinking gift and Ellen has the Intuitive gift, neither of them has the special combination of Intuition and Thinking (NT) that the pastor shares with only about 20% of males and 9% of the females in Myers's study.

An NT tends to be intellectual, logical, and ingenious. Understandably, NTs are attracted to jobs where they can use their analytical ability. Executive management, computer systems analysis, science, and law are some of the vocations where sizable numbers of NTs are found. They have a natural ability to do long-range planning and find problems stimulating. An NT like Margie's pastor would not for a moment entertain any serious doubt that the congregation could rise to the challenge that the industrial park represented.

NTs and the church

Like NFs, NTs have an Intuitive perception that enables them to see the "big picture." They are stimulated by complexity and enjoy seeing how everything fits together in patterns. They differ from NFs in that they do not use Feeling judgment in making decisions about what they see, preferring instead to analyze a problem and come to a logical conclusion. NTs tend to take a long-range view of things and have the ability to look at a situation as if they were an objective observer. Because they take feelings into consideration only when it is logical to do so, NTs can be misperceived as personally detached or even aloof. However, their more impersonal approach to situations is not intended to be distant. It is rather the approach that a Thinking type believes will keep personal bias from getting in the way of the best resolution of a problem.

ENTJ

An extraverted and organized NT like Margie's pastor (ENTJ: approximately 5% of males and 2% of the females in Myers' high school study), is a person who likes to bring about change. Rising to administrative positions in many fields, an ENTJ brings a "take charge" and "can do" attitude to almost any task. By seeing possibilities and demonstrating good organizational ability, a mature ENTJ not only has confidence but inspires confidence in others. Because Thinking is an ENTJ's primary gift, there is always the possibility that the feeling side of life may be less developed, resulting in an ENTJ unintentionally overlooking the feelings of others. For the pastor, it will be important to realize that for some people there may be strong emotional attachments to the way things have been in the past that will have to be addressed before there can be wholehearted support of the new directions the pastor wants to propose.

In conversation, an ENTJ may be so engrossed in surfacing ideas and posing possibilities that the listener feels overwhelmed. However, it is not the intention of an ENTJ to monopolize a conversation. It is simply the ENTJ's way of thinking through a problem by talking it through. Most of what may sound like conclusions are really only ideas being checked out. Dialog is welcome. Entering into such discussions gives an ENTJ an opportunity to explore all sides of a question. Through the give and take of discussion, an ENTJ can provide forward-looking leadership in many areas of congregational life.

INTJ

If instead of being extraverted an NTJ is *Introverted* (*I*NTJ: perhaps 4% of males and 1% of females, Myers), that person will probably have a strong, intuitive grasp of what is possible, an inner vision that the individual longs to see worked out in practice. Like an ENTJ, the INTJ is also an administrative type, but is usually a more reflective leader, developing designs but not necessarily wanting to be the person who implements them. Science, law, computer systems, psychology, and many other professions attract an INTJ. In the congregation, long-range planning committees or a task force charged with analyzing the strengths and weaknesses of congregational activities might be of great interest. As with all NTs, it is helpful if an INTJ gives conscious attention to the feelings of others and makes a deliberate effort to express appreciation for what others do.

INTP

An Introverted NT who is *Perceptive* rather than Judging (INTP: about 5% of males and 2% of females, Myers) brings to the congregation a special gift of logically ordering ideas and knowledge. INTPs use Intuition in the outer world. They are curious and interested in many things. They then reflect on those things by using their primary gift of analytical thought. Scientists, researchers, mathematicians, engineers, economists, and philosophers are among the vocations that are satisfying to those with this gift. In a congregational setting, an INTP, like most other NTs, will be able to take an idea and carefully analyze it to see where the flaws are to be found. Consequently, program review and development may be of interest to INTPs. They may also be good problem solvers, coming up with highly ingenious solutions for complicated situations.

ENTP

When an NTP is *Extraverted* (ENTP: about 6% of male and 3% of female high school students in Myers' research), it is Intuition that is the principal gift, and it is used in the outside world of people and things. An ENTP brings a lot of imagination into the church, and probably will be interested in getting a number of projects started. In their work they want to do something that is challenging, and they prefer to go from one challenge to another. Marketing and journalism provide needed stimulation for ENTPs, but they can see opportunity in almost any field that does not require doing the same thing over and over. In congregational settings, an ENTP might make a very innovative planner, but he or she might be happier staying with a project only long enough to get it well under way, then move to another assignment.

Appreciating and supporting an NT

Do you have the NT gift? Does someone in your family or in your congregation have that gift? Like the NFs, there do not seem to be as many persons gifted as NTs as there are STs and SFs. About 15% of the people in Myers' study reported a preference for NT. This includes NTs in any of the four ways the NT gift is expressed: INTJ, INTP, ENTP, and ENTJ. Probably among those persons you know well there are some who would find their place in the last column of the Type Table:

ISTJ	ISFJ	INFJ	**INTJ**
ISTP	ISFP	INFP	**INTP**
ESTP	ESFP	ENFP	**ENTP**
ESTJ	ESFJ	ENFJ	**ENTJ**

Based on your reading of "The Strengths of an NT"

and "NTs and the Church," use the descriptions to help you answer these questions:

Has God gifted someone in your family as an NT? If you think God has, pencil in their names:

Circle one, if possible

_____ (INTJ, INTP, ENTP, ENTJ)

_____ (INTJ, INTP, ENTP, ENTJ)

Has God gifted someone at work/school/etc. as an NT?

Circle one, if possible

_____ (INTJ, INTP, ENTP, ENTJ)

_____ (INTJ, INTP, ENTP, ENTJ)

Has God gifted someone in your congregation as an NT?

Circle one, if possible

_____ (INTJ, INTP, ENTP, ENTJ)

_____ (INTJ, INTP, ENTP, ENTJ)

An Intuitive Thinker is gifted by God in a very special way. As is true for persons with any of the personality gifts, NTs appreciate it when their gifts are respected by fellow Christians. Sometimes a misperception of the NT gets in the way of this appreciation. As we have seen earlier, at times the intellectual bent of NTs, combined with their tendency to overlook the feeling side of life, results in their being considered cool and aloof. However, those who have engaged an NT in a passionate exchange of ideas can testify that the NT is far from detached! It is rather that their Thinking gift sharpens the issues for them in a way that enables them to focus on principles rather than persons. The exchange of ideas is stimulating for NTs, and they consider such exchanges valuable, whether or not they agree with the person they are talking to. If needed support is to be given, it is important not to misperceive an NT.

To know how to provide support for an NT, let's take one more look at the whole person model as it applies to those whom God has gifted with Intuition and Thinking. As whole persons, an NT is more likely to neglect the physical and emotional dimensions of life. *Physically* the NT (with all other Intuitives) has to take care not to overlook basic bodily needs. Finding a balance between a healthy mind and a healthy body is a challenge for all Christians, but even more so for those whose personality leads them to exercise their minds much more than they exercise their bodies. Fellow Christians, especially those with a Sensing appreciation of the physical, may be able to encourage an Intuitive Thinker to remember to be a good steward of God's gift of the body.

It might not seem that an NT would need much support in the *intellectual* area, but sometimes persons gifted with Intuition and Thinking are not given as much opportunity to use their gifts in congregations as they might. Because they are analytical and critical thinkers, they may be quicker than most to identify what is wrong and so may not always be perceived as the most cooperative of members. In fact, they are usually eager to contribute, especially in areas of congregational thinking or envisioning that utilize their gifts. It is unfortunate that sometimes their ability to analyze a situation is not called into play until church members are talking about what went wrong in a congregational program. It would be both more supportive and better stewardship of gifts to give NTs the chance to provide advice and assistance in advance of the implementation of a program, so things have a better chance of going well.

An NT can be a real asset on long-range planning and congregational strategy committees, as well as in putting together adult education and social action programs. The commitment of most NTs to social justice issues is very strong and they are often articulate spokespersons for worthy causes.

As we have seen, the *feeling* dimension for many NTs tends to be less available to them. The quickness of their minds often results in NTs discussing issues rather intensely. They become so engaged in the interplay of ideas that they may not pick up signs of discomfort or uneasiness in their conversation partner or in a group. It may be helpful to the NT if others will point out the presence of any negative feelings in a straightforward, factual way so that the NT can take those feelings more fully into consideration. It can be especially supportive if others make the assumption that NTs are not intending any personal offense in what they say, even if they have strong differences of opinion with others. Feeling types may find it hard to understand how they do it, but an NT can relatively easily separate a difference of opinion from personal feelings. While NTs will be well-advised to check out the feelings of those with whom they disagree, it is supportive to give them the benefit of the doubt as to their intentions.

Socially, as with the other possible combinations of personality preferences, an NT's orientation to the world as an Extravert or Intravert will have something to do with his or her comfort in social situations. In either case, what will help is for NTs to develop the feeling side of their personalities so that their caring comes through a little more clearly. Others can help by reinforcing NTs' efforts in these less natural directions, letting them know that what they are trying to do feels good and is appreciated. It is also helpful for others not to assume that NTs, especially Introverted NTs, do not want or need meaningful relationships. But you may have to take the initiative if you want to have a relationship with them.

The *spiritual* life of an NT may be nurtured in many ways. Preaching, of course, needs to point to universal truths that apply in all times and in all places. NTs are interested in abstractions and may be most stimulated if they are left to fill in some of the blanks—as long as the underlying structure of the sermon is solid and thought-provoking. Education, of course, needs to have that same depth and soundness, and an NT may profitably be challenged to make some independent inquiries or do some further research in between classes. Intuitive Thinking persons are especially attracted to education as a way to express their Christian discipleship. It is more through learning than through mysticism or some other more personal and subjective experience that most NTs find their relationship with God nurtured. A spiritual path based on learning rather than feelings is a preferred path for the majority of NTs, since it reflects their natural gifts and strengths.

In worship, an NT may prefer having a liturgical structure to the service, or at least having some organizing principle that has continuity over time without being routine. Prayers that have been prayed throughout the ages may be more appealing than more personal petitions. An NT does not usually have a "Jesus and me" approach to personal piety. That seems to be too individualistic to most NTs. Rather, an NT will usually feel most satisfied with worship if he or she leaves the sanctuary with an awareness of being connected with the Author of the faith and with all those who look to the eternal God as a refuge and strength.

If your pastor appears to be an NT, you may find the general description of the "Strengths of an NT" and "NTs and the Church" helpful. Since Margie's pastor is an Intuitive Thinking type, that story may give you some additional insight into how an NT pastor approaches situations. Perhaps it is most important that you find a way to appreciate and support the visionary leadership of your pastor. Those visions for the congregation have to be informed by facts and, of course, by whatever practical limitations exist. But an NT pastor will consider it supportive if the congregation first tries to listen to the potential rather than immediately focus on why the plan or program will not work. With that kind of response, Margie's pastor would then be encouraged to get a group working on what options and alternatives are available to the congregation. As an NT, Margie's pastor would also be very open to having the pros and cons of each of those alternatives aired.

An NT pastor will probably be more conscious of social issues and broader socio-cultural concerns than many in the congregation. Since NTs characteristically think in terms of systems, that includes *social* systems. With their capacity to spot flaws in systems, they are likely to see where a social system is not working very well. It is very important to have this kind of voice raised in the church. In some cases it may be a prophetic voice that challenges and confronts injustices where they are found. An NT pastor will provide a valuable service to the congregation in keeping the eyes of the congregation lifted up to God's purposes for all humankind. Their vision of the future and what the church can be enables them to provide effective ministry in the present.

Sharing the NT gift

An Intuitive Thinking pastor or layperson has many gifts to bring to the Christian church, gifts that can be instrumental in lifting a congregation's eyes to the universal priesthood of all believers and to the Christ as, in the book of Colossians, a Christ of all creation (Col. 1:15-29).

As with each of the other gifts, to appreciate and support those gifted with Intuition and Thinking is the first way to share in the blessings of this gift. By appreciating and supporting them, we encourage NTs to offer their gift for the part that gift can play in the equipping of the saints for the work of ministry and the upbuilding of the body of Christ. We have already pointed out that Feeling persons will have to trust that while an NT may have a less personal manner that does not mean he or she is uncaring. Once other Christians perceive the kind of caring that is the gift of an NT, and the valuable contribution an NT can make to serious discussions, then the Christian community will eagerly affirm those whom God has blessed with Intuitive Thinking. Through the NT gift (as with all the gifts) the entire church is strengthened.

We can do more than simply appreciate and support the NT gift in others. It is also possible to cultivate that way of looking at life within ourselves. This is probably a little easier for persons with NF and ST gifts. The point of intersection with NF is the fact that both NTs and NFs share the common gift of Intuition. Because of their Intuition, Intuitive Feeling persons are usually able to communicate quite easily with NTs. They tend to perceive things in similar ways. To share the NT gift, however, an NF will need to set aside temporarily the personally meaningful values that usually guide NF decision making. Instead, the person who usually prefers Feeling judgment will want to look at the situation (or decision) as an individual would who is less personally involved. An NT analysis of the issues takes into account the pros and cons of each possible solution, as well as all the possible consequences of each decision as best they can be known. The guideline for NT decision making is reliance on principles that have stood and can continue to stand the test of time.

A Sensing Thinking type (ST) already approaches situations and decisions with logical analysis (T), so to share the gift of the NT requires not a different way of thinking but a different way of looking at the situation to begin with. Along with gathering information with Sensing, which focuses on the specific facts in the here and now, an ST must look at how those facts intuitively fit together to form a pattern—a larger picture. An ST has a practical and realistic gift. To grow in the use of the gift of an NT means growing in the ability to let go of what is known long enough to get a good idea of what might be. This leaving of the known facts is not a natural inclination for an ST. However, just as Thinking can complement Feeling, so an Intuitive approach can complement a Sensing approach to problems. Each is one of God's good gifts.

It is the Sensing Feeling person (SF) who is likely to have the hardest time fully appreciating an NT. This is because an SF shares neither an NT's Intuition nor an NT's Thinking. An NT approach will probably be thought of as far too removed from the concrete and practical, personal realities of everyday life that are an SF's primary concern. An SF might go so far as to say that what seems to preoccupy an NT is, for the most part, simply irrelevant to day-to-day life.

However negative that impression seems to be, there are some reasons for it. An NT and an SF typically hold different things to be of fundamental importance. In addition, a negative reaction can be set up if an SF in some way feels intimidated by a NT. Often an NT excels in academic studies, and an SF—especially extraverted SFs—may not. This does not mean that an NT is necessarily more intelligent than an SF, since academic studies are often taught in such a way as to favor an NT. Unfortunately and mistakenly, an SF may mistake the difference in classroom performance as a difference in native intelligence.

While the SF gift is as truly a gift as that given to the NT, there is a person-centered reason for an SF to try to share some of what comes naturally to an Intuitive Thinking Type. An SF is very concerned about the welfare of individual persons. It is helpful for an SF to consider how much more good could be done for individuals if some of the larger social and systemic problems of our culture were solved. The gift of an NT is to look at those larger patterns in as unbiased a way as possible in an effort to search out more just resolutions to problems. To share the gift of NTs will require that SFs move beyond concrete situations, but only long enough to be able to return to their more familiar world with additional perspectives that may make a difference to one of those persons who desperately needs help.

For persons with one gift to try to share the gift given to someone else requires an awareness of what the differences are and a belief that each of our different approaches to life is valuable. The Bible invites us to expect that people will have different gifts. God's Word also asks that each of those gifts be used—effectively and faithfully.

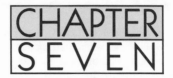

CHAPTER SEVEN

Having Gifts
That Differ . . .
Let Us Use Them

Throughout this book we have been talking about gifts, different gifts given to us by God. But in the book of Romans Paul asks that we do more than just recognize our gifts. We are to *use* those gifts to the glory of God (12:6). Ephesians 4:12 says our individual gifts are to be used "to equip the saints for the work of ministry, for building up the body of Christ." In this way our diversity, which is a gift of God, enriches and strengthens our unity as the people of God.

If we are to use our gifts to do the work of ministry, it is reasonable for us to ask just what that ministry is. The Bible provides us with a number of answers to that question. In the Old Testament, Micah talked about ministry as doing justice, loving kindness, and walking humbly with our God (Mic. 6:8). In the books of Matthew and Acts, ministry is understood as telling the good news of the gospel to all the world (Matt. 28:19-20; Acts 6:4; 20:24). But for me, one of the most meaningful descriptions of the ministry of Christian men and women is what Paul described in 2 Corinthians 5. Once again, Paul proclaimed the good news of our reconciliation to God through Jesus Christ. Then Paul went on to say that to us who have been reconciled has been given a ministry, "the ministry of reconciliation" (2 Cor. 5:18).

There are many ways to fulfill our ministry of reconciliation. Bringing persons to Jesus Christ is, of course, the basic foundation. The ministry of reconciliation, as Paul understood it, grows out of the relationship with God that Christ makes possible. Evangelism has at its heart the telling of this good news (gospel) of what God has done for us. In faithfulness to its calling, the church wants as many people as possible to hear the story of salvation. We do not simply wait for people to come to us to hear the story. We take the good news *to* them. The ministry of reconciliation is not only our ministry, it is also our *mission* as God's reconciled people.

However, the good news of reconciliation is not only to be proclaimed from the pulpit or to be at the heart of our evangelistic outreach. An equally strong testimony to the message of reconciliation is found in the way we Christians live out our lives. As new persons in Christ, our way of going about our relationships with others is perhaps our strongest witness to the power of the reconciling love of God.

It is in this respect that the MBTI can be of special help to the Christian community. In her book *Gifts Differing* (with Peter Myers, Consulting Psychologists Press, 1980), Isabel Briggs Myers pointed out that many of the conflicts between people come about as a result of our lack of appreciation of the fact that people have been gifted differently. That which we do not understand very often puts us off. It confuses us and may offend or threaten us. Myers believed that an understanding of our differing gifts would guide people in their efforts to have more caring relationships with each other.

Let's see how the Myers-Briggs perspective might help us to avoid conflict in two different kinds of situations. First, we'll look at how MBTI insights might be useful in avoiding conflict in the interpersonal relationship between Mike and Ellen, since they have such different personality gifts. Then we'll turn to how the Myers-Briggs can be of help in dealing with typical congregational conflicts over worship.

Using our gifts for reconciling relationships

Many married men and women at one time or another get to a place where they feel that they are very much misunderstood and unappreciated. When people feel like that, they also often believe that their partner has failed them in some way.

As a couple married for 18 years, Mike and Ellen have had their share of times when they felt misunderstood and let down by each other, times when each thought the other had failed to be sensitive and caring. One such time was when Mike proposed the move to Fairvue so he could advance at his company. When Mike presented the idea he seemed so intent on making the move that Ellen at first sat on her negative feelings about relocating. Over and over Ellen reviewed in her mind all her reasons for wanting to stay put, but she held back from speaking her mind out loud. One thing she knew for certain was that, as far as she was concerned, Mike had been insensitive. How could he not realize how important her teaching position was to her?

But that was only one of the times their relationship had become rocky over the years. There were many other times when their communication faltered and they felt "unreconciled." Some years earlier, when their old car broke down, they had to make a decision whether or not to fix it or buy a newer one. Buying a newer car would mean using up the savings they had set aside for Ellen to begin a masters degree program that she wanted very much to complete. It was a difficult decision and resulted in some unpleasant arguments. As a Christian couple it bothered them to realize that their relationship was not perfect, but the reality was that they often fell short of the way they wished their marriage could be.

If as a spouse we point out the way our husband or wife has let us down—and especially if we do it in an attacking way—it often leads only to our partner becoming defensive. But there is another way of dealing with these failures in our relationships that makes it possible for a relationship to be both reconciled and strengthened.

The key lies in how a couple perceives the situation when things are going poorly between them. One of the reasons Ellen keeps quiet is that she sees problems primarily as a threat to her relationship with Mike. A Christian couple can deal with their relational failures more faithfully if they try also to see their problem as a challenge and an opportunity to make their marriage better. What is it that transforms a marital problem into a challenging opportunity? It is the presence of Christ in our hearts and in our marriages and his promise that he is with us! If we truly believe that Christ is present and cares about what we are going through, then we also believe that he will be able to lift us up and help us look at our situation with new eyes. "Behold, I make all things new!" (Rev. 21:5).

How does God give us the ability to look at things anew? It happens differently for different people. One couple may be able to see the old in a new way because of something that their pastor says during a sermon; for another it may be an insight that comes while one or both are in Bible study; for another it may be an answer that comes during prayer. But sometimes God works indirectly. Perhaps a chance comment by a coworker will stimulate a husband or wife to look at their situation in a new and more positive way. Or perhaps a counselor will provide a different perspective on their situation.

Another way we can look at old problems with new eyes is with the help of the MBTI, understood as a way of helping us discover and use our God-given gifts. If we use this perspective on the problems Mike and Ellen experience, we begin to see that some of what causes conflict in their marriage is neither ill will nor hard-heartedness, but the natural expression of different God-given personality gifts that they had failed to understand. And what we do not understand we often fail to appreciate.

In our description of Mike and Ellen we learned that Mike has personality preferences for Extraversion, Sensing, Thinking, and Judging (ESTJ). Ellen is Introverted, Intuitive, Feeling, and Perceptive (INFP). We can see at a glance that Mike and Ellen do not have one letter in common between their two personality types!

Mike, being Extraverted, gets his energy from interacting with the outer world of people and things. As a Sensing person, he uses his senses of sight, sound, hearing, taste, and touch to keep himself very much aware of the details of day-to-day living. What is happening in the here and now is what is important to him. Being a Thinking person, Mike prefers to make decisions on the basis of logical analysis, not primarily on how that decision will affect people. He tries to be objective and to weigh the facts fairly. As a Judging person, Mike is orderly and organized. He likes to plan ahead and stay with that plan.

But an INFP has quite different preferences. Being Introverted means that Ellen's energy comes not from the outside world but from the inner world of thoughts and ideas. Being an Intuitive, she relies not so much on the five senses as she does on a sixth sense or impression of how all the pieces of a particular situation fit together in a pattern of meaning. Her inclination to see where things are going in terms of a emerging pattern causes Ellen to be more oriented toward the future than toward the present. When a decision has to be made, Ellen decides on the basis of personal and interpersonal values: what is important to people—herself and others. The *P* at the end of INFP means that instead of orderliness and organization, Ellen prefers a Perceptive life-style, one that is marked by flexibility and adaptability—as long as one of her basic values is not at stake.

Let's now apply an understanding of personality gifts to the kinds of problems Mike and Ellen have faced during their marriage, problems which many marriages have experienced from time to time. It will help if we keep in mind that most marriage counselors report that there are certain areas that become problem spots for many couples, and Mike and Ellen are no exception. The problem areas include arguments over finances or material possessions, different approaches to decision making, dissatisfaction with the level of emotional and sexual intimacy, and breakdowns in communication.

If we look at each of these typical tension areas with personality type in mind, we can soon see that personality preferences play a very important role in a marriage. For example, the importance one places on material possessions varies depending on whether you are a Sensing person or an Intuitive person. As a Sensing person, Mike wants to make the present life situation as pleasant and comfortable as possible. God has gifted him with a delight in the bounty of the present: "This is the day which the Lord has made; let us rejoice and be glad in it" (Ps. 118:24). For Mike, setting aside the present for a possible future does not seem to be a good way to live.

Intuitive Ellen, however, can delay present pleasures for extended periods of time without giving a thought to what is being set aside, because the pull of the future is so strong: "forgetting what lies behind and straining forward to what lies ahead" (Phil. 3:13). For Ellen, a car was a car, whatever its age and however it looked. Education, however, really meant something. It was building for the future. For Mike, good, reliable transportation was a practical necessity and a pressing need, and a newer car would make for fewer problems in the long run. The marriage problem came when neither Mike nor Ellen appreciated the gift of the other. Ellen then perceived Mike as being *overly* concerned with physical things and the here and now, even materialistic. On the other hand, Mike perceived Ellen as being inattentive or even disinterested in what was needed by the family for day-to-day living.

A biblically based understanding of personality gifts can help a Christian couple understand that both the Sensing and the Intuitive ways of perceiving are God-given gifts. And each gift needs the other. In Mike and Ellen's relationship, Mike needs Ellen to help him see beyond the present moment and look for larger meanings in life. Ellen needs Mike's openness to the blessings each day brings and needs to learn the joy of living one day at a time. In marriages where both of the spouses are Sensing or both of the partners are Intuitives, they may see things the same way more often, but their challenge will be to be sure that the "missing" way of seeing finds a proper place in their relationship. It is important to remember that *there are no "incompatible" personality types.* Each combination has its own problems and its own possibilities. *The key is how each couple perceives their mutual gifts, and how they make use of them to the glory of God.*

Decision making is another area of contention for many couples, as it was for Mike and Ellen. This is an area where a Judgment/Perception difference between marriage partners can pose some problems. Because Mike prefers an organized and orderly life, he likes to get decisions out of the way. Moses once said to the people of

Israel: "I have set before you life and death, blessing and curse; therefore choose life ..." (Deut. 30:19). While this passage primarily has to do with obedient faithfulness to God, one of the ways we express this faithfulness is in the way we go about making decisions. Mike's way of "choosing life" is to consider what needs to be done and make the appropriate decision. Decisions put closure on an area and make it possible for him to get on with the rest of life. Ellen has a different way of looking at decisions. For her, making a final decision closes off options and opportunities. Her way of "choosing life" is to keep the door open for new information and new possibilities.

What can happen in a marriage is that the partner who likes closure can see his or her spouse as indecisive or a procrastinator. On the other hand, a Perceptive partner may think that the Judging spouse is making a premature, insufficiently considered choice. In both of Mike and Ellen's decisions (whether or not to make a move and whether or not to buy a newer car) they disagreed not only on which decision was "right," but also on how soon they should decide.

Both the Judging and the Perceiving personality gifts actually bring a special strength to times of decision. Ellen's Perceptive gift of keeping options open helps her and Mike to stay with the problem long enough to understand what the issues are. Mike helps them come to a place where they stop processing the problem and actually decide one way or another. When couples run into trouble in the decision-making area of their marriage, they may want to ask themselves whether or not they are balancing the gift of remaining open with the gift of bringing things to a close and putting the past behind them.

How couples handle their problems has a lot to do with how close they feel, and intimacy is another area where personality differences can create problems. Like many couples, Mike and Ellen have a Thinking-Feeling difference that they have to learn to use constructively. Mike has strong principles and tries to apply them evenly. He analyzes what needs to be done and then does it. Ellen sees the value of Mike's dedication to the task and to principles, but at times experiences him as unfeeling and uncaring, as she did when he first proposed moving to Fairvue. When Ellen is hurting from the potential loss of her friends and teaching colleagues, what she wants is not an analysis of the situation but comfort and support. From Mike's perspective, however, Ellen is inclined to allow her feelings to take over and get in the way of her making "sensible" decisions.

A couple's intimacy and sexual relationship can be affected if either marital partner fails to appreciate the gift that the other brings to the relationship. If what looks like insensitivity on the part of Mike can be understood more positively and appreciated, then it does not have to be a barrier to closeness. Mike does care, but he will more naturally show his caring in a Thinking person's way. On the other hand, if what looks like emotionality on the part of Ellen is understood and appreciated, then it is no block to real dialog and the sharing of ideas. Feeling persons use their head every bit as well as Thinking persons, they just work through problems with a different rationale and a different set of values.

Intimacy is a matter of both the heart and the mind, and sex is simply the expression of this closeness in physical terms. When marriage partners feel let down by one another, feel uncared about and misunderstood, then they are likely to be less satisfied with their sexual relationship and more vulnerable to attractions outside the marriage. In some marriages, it may be work that becomes the mistress, but the dynamics are similar regardless of what or who the "third party" is. And the challenge for the couple is clear.

If both Thinking and Feeling are gifts from God, then both need to be integrated into the marriage relationship. A failure to find a balance between the Thinking and Feeling side of a marriage is likely to lead to conflict and estrangement, and this is especially true if there is poor communication.

Some marriage counselors say that where there is good communication between the partners, almost any marriage problem can be solved. The difference in personality preference that seems to have the most direct effect on communication is a difference in preference for Extraversion or Introversion.

Returning to Mike's and Ellen's relationship, Mike's extraverted way of communicating is to talk out loud. As a matter of fact, most Extraverts *think* out loud. When Extraverts hear themselves say things to other people, this helps them clarify their understanding and leads them to a conviction, or perhaps to a change of mind.

Ellen's way of communicating is quite different from Mike's. As an Introvert, she keeps her thinking process inside—reflecting, weighing, considering. Only when some conclusions have been reached is she ready to share her thoughts out loud. To some Extraverts, introverted partners may seem withdrawn and uncommunicative.

What appear to be failures in communication may simply be the lack of a couple's awareness that Extraverts and Introverts have two very different communication styles. When there are breakdowns in communication, it is helpful for a couple to ask whether only one style is being used or valued. A good way for Mike to get an idea of what Ellen is thinking and feeling is simply to ask— and then really listen. A good way for Ellen to keep the lines of communication open with Mike is not to jump in too quickly to counter what he is saying, because the chances are pretty good that what Mike has just said is not really a conclusion but his out-loud thinking process. Here again, it helps to ask.

At the heart of many of the problems we have discussed is a difference in values. Extraverts value some things differently than Introverts, Sensing persons see things differently than Intuitives, Thinking persons use different criteria in making decisions than Feeling persons, and Judging persons value order and organization in a way that Perceptives do not. Just as diversity is sometimes viewed negatively in the church, the diversity that exists between Christian couples can be, and sometimes is, perceived as a problem, a letting down of each other. When relational conflicts are not understood, they can lead to anger and estrangement.

A step toward reconciliation comes when we allow our faith to help us see that many of our differences have nothing to do with "right" or "wrong." They simply arise out of the fact that we have different God-given gifts, each one of which is in itself good because it comes from God. But our differing gifts are not given in order that we might prevail over someone else. One of the points at which sin enters our relationships is in the misuse of our personality gifts. To absolutize our gift, that is, to believe that our preferred way is *the* way, and our preferred "truth" is the *only* truth, is to fall to the same temptation that Adam and Eve faced in the Garden of Eden—to try to be like God.

Instead, each of us is to use God's gift to us, recognizing the strengths that our gift offers—and also its limitations. At the theological level, what we must do is accept our finitude—accept the fact that we are *not* God. Not being God means that we are not sufficient in and of ourselves. Since God created us with different gifts, we really need each other if our life and experience and witness is to be more complete. To accept ourselves and others in this way is to let our diversity become an opportunity for us to grow in understanding and appreciation of one another and of our relationship to God. When estranged people bring this kind of spirit into their conflict, reconciliation may not be far behind.

Using our gifts to glorify God

For Christians there is probably no hour more talked about during the week than the worship hour. Discussions range from how the sermon was to what hymns were sung, how long the prayers were, whether or not the choir seemed well-rehearsed and on key, and whether or not the hour stretched to 65 minutes (or more).

Not long ago an article caught my eye. Its title was "Reducing Warfare over Worship." While the article was written by a pastor and intended for pastors, the message applies to laypersons equally as well. The basic point was that people have different preferences in worship. The potential for "warfare" over worship increases when one person's personal preference is pushed onto others. The article went on to suggest how Myers-Briggs preferences for Sensing and Intuition result in differing approaches to worship and potential conflict in a congregation. Warfare over worship can be reduced when preferences are understood as *preferences*, and when there is appreciation and respect for those preferences that are not our own.

In each of the chapters of this book, one of the spiritual implications we discussed was the way different MBTI preferences lead persons to take different approaches to worship. However, in order to speak accurately about the spiritual implications of the Myers-Briggs we need to look more closely at the whole area of spirituality.

It is helpful first to distinguish three words that are sometimes used interchangeably: *spiritual, spirituality,* and *spiritual discipline* or *expression.* I believe the best definition of the word *spiritual* is based on Eph. 3:14-19:

> For this reason I bow my knees before [God], from whom every family in heaven and on earth is named, that according to the riches of [God's glory God] may grant you to be strengthened with might through [the] Spirit in the inner [person], and that Christ may dwell in your hearts through faith; that you, being rooted and grounded in love, may have power to comprehend with all the saints what is the breadth and length and height and depth, and to know the love of Christ which surpasses knowledge, that you may be filled with all the fullness of God.

For me, the *spiritual* (Spirit-ual) is the heighth, length, breadth, and depth of the love of God that underlies, embraces, and transforms our personal and communal life together. Christians believe that God's love has been most clearly and gracefully revealed in Christ Jesus. Note that the symbol of the cross is created vertically (height and depth) and horizontally (length and breadth). The spiritual nature of life is not ours to design or develop. It is a gift of God.

When we remember that *all* of life is a gift of the Spirit, then it is not possible to understand spirituality as a *part* of our life. *Spirituality* is really an *orientation* to life. Spirituality grows out of our individual and corporate perception and reception of the spiritual as the integrating center of the physical, mental, emotional, and social dimensions of our lives. As a cognitive perception, we might say that spirituality is "seeing with the eyes of faith." On the feeling side, as one theologian has said, spirituality is "accepting our acceptance by God."

Our spirituality, however, is not fully integrated and focused unless it finds faithful expression. *Spiritual discipline* or *spiritual expression* are terms that describe the ways that believing persons and communities nurture and *reflect* their spirituality. Because people are gifted differently, and have different personal histories and life situations, it is to be expected that they may find different ways of expressing their response to God. Moreover, the forms with which persons express their spirituality may change and develop over time (although those forms need not change—they may simply deepen) Finally, alongside meaningful individual expressions of spirituality, there are corporate expressions. We know that the Judeo-Christian community throughout the ages has expressed its spirituality in the study of Scripture and in prayer, praise, and thanksgiving as a people of God. The Christian church traditionally nurtures spirituality through the Word of God, baptism, and the Lord's Supper.

From the standpoint of faith, the spiritual is the given nature of life. It precedes the personality types that are identified by the Myers-Briggs. However, because personality type has to do with the way we perceive, and spirituality is at least in part a cognitive perception, personality type may play a part in what we are most likely to "see" with "the eyes of faith." For example, the Sensing person may be the one most easily able to perceive the presence of God in the physical, sensory world, and the Feeling person may more quickly "see" the spiritual reflected in human relationships.

However, because the interrelationships between personality type and spirituality may be subtle and difficult to discern, the effect of personality type is probably most clearly evident in how different persons prefer to *nurture* and *express* their spirituality. The forms of worship that appeal to us (or the absence of any formal structure)—whether we like to sing emotionally-moving or mentally stimulating hymns, our preference either for formal or free-form prayer, the use of simple stories or technical theological concepts in the sermon, the quiet and reflective or active and socializing character of the worship service—all these are *expressions* of our spirituality that are greatly affected by personality preferences.

If Mike and Ellen were both members of the worship committee of their congregation, it is highly unlikely that they would agree on how the church's worship should be conducted. Extraverted Mike would probably enjoy having a time set aside during the worship service for the members to go around the congregation greeting people. Introverted Ellen would probably *respond* to those who approached her with outstretched hand, but she would not likely move too far from her seat to *initiate* contact with anyone she did not know pretty well. Mike might prefer plain-spoken, straightforward sermons that have a clear beginning, middle, and end, and he might appreciate some specific, practical applications—as most Sensing parishioners do. Ellen may be more inspired by the pastor's use of images and metaphors that communicate the main idea without spelling out the implications in great detail. Intuitives like to make their own connections.

Mike may not expect to be personally moved by the choir selections, but he would like them to be carefully chosen, well-rehearsed, and technically well-presented. Ellen's more Feeling nature looks for music to evoke or at least resonate with her inner feelings and values. As a member of a worship committee, Mike would very likely be concerned about the "packaging" of the worship service: whether or not it starts and ends on time, how orderly and organized it is, and how efficiently and effectively the various parts of the service fit together. While it might not necessarily be the worship committee's responsibility, he would probably also pay attention to how this year's attendance compares to last year's and how the offerings are holding up compared with congregational expenses. Ellen may be more interested in the general "feel" of the worship hour and whether or not there is enough flexibility in the congregation's approach to worship to allow for spontaneity.

Which of these approaches to worship is "correct" or "more Christian"? If you have an answer to that question, you might want to check to see if your answer lies in the direction of your own personality preferences! A biblically-based understanding of the differing gifts God has given us would suggest that there is no one "correct" worship standard for all Christians. God has chosen to gift us differently, and each of those gifts can be used to glorify God.

At the heart of congregational conflict over worship practices may lie a failure fully to appreciate the richness that God's differing gifts bestow on the church. Reconciliation lies in the direction of Christians realizing that the *spiritual* and *spiritual expression* are not the same thing. The spiritual nature of life is a gracious reality that proceeds from God the Creator, Redeemer, and Sanctifier. We cannot create such a spiritual reality, we can only accept it (or turn away from it).

The relationship of Christian worship to the spiritual is therefore *responsive*. Worship is our grateful response to God. Our most genuine spiritual expression of our gratitude for God's grace will come out of the depth of our being. Depending on how God has individually gifted us, we may find one rather than another spiritual expression or discipline to be the "best" way for us to say "thank you" to God. An inclusive church will be sensitive to the variety of gifts that are present among the people of God. And an inclusive church knows the importance of finding ways to affirm each of God's gifts in the context of the corporate "thank you" to God that we express in worship.

Practically speaking, this means that many conflicts over worship can be seen more accurately as disagreements over which personal preferences are to be followed in a given situation. Elevating preferences to the level of "right or wrong" not only makes reconciliation more difficult, it also absolutizes our personal preferences in a way even God chose not to do.

By saying that many conflicts over worship can be seen in more proper perspective as conflicts over personal preferences, *I am not in any way suggesting* that sound theology and specific worship practices have nothing to do with each other. The form of our worship always needs faithfully to express the dynamic of our faith. One of the blessings of a church is that there is a community of faith that has both a history (a tradition) and a readiness to help individual Christians check out their personal perceptions to see if they are consistent with the church's basic beliefs. But the fact remains that many conflicts over worship among Christians can be seen in an entirely different light when *what is at stake is not the basic beliefs of the church but rather people's personal preferences.* In those situations, having a solid theology of gifts can enable Christians to take the needed steps toward reconciliation.

Using our gifts for mission

As you have read this book I hope you have found a new awareness of and a heightened appreciation for your own personal gifts. You are one of God's gifted people! God is counting on you to use your gifts in ways that will "equip the saints" at home, at work, in your congregation, and in the world. Almost everything we have said about the use of our gifts in our everyday, "close-to-home" lives can be applied also to the wider community, to God's children everywhere. For example, what we have discussed in relation to congregational conflicts over worship has some relevance for improving relationships among the various Christian denominations. Some of the things that look like barriers between different denominations do not seem so insumountable when they are understood as the expression of differing gifts and preferences.

You may also be able to see some ways in which a theology of gifts helps us in our interfaith dialog with non-Christians all over the globe. All people are created in God's image and are gifted in one way or another. Each has a perspective to share that is worth hearing. Cross-cultural experience suggests that the predominant personality types in one country may not be the same as the predominant personality types in other parts of the world. Is it possible that God has gifted not only different people but different *peoples* in different ways as a reminder of our interdependence and need for one another? Along with their personality gifts, people of other cultures may also give us a gift that leads to our own growth in the Spirit. As we learn from stories in the Bible, sometimes it is through the stranger, the one who does not belong to our own community of faith, that God raises to our attention a possibility or speaks to us a word that is very important for us to hear.

When I use my gifts to listen carefully to others—even to those outside the faith—I may hear something that will help me be a more effective witness for Christ. If we take time to listen to those who do not know Christ we will hear them raising very fundamental human questions—questions that most of us have had and some which we may still have. People everywhere search for the meaning and purpose of life, and they are looking for a way to relate these larger questions to everyday life. A Christian witness to Jesus Christ will be more effective when we do not pronounce God's answer before we are sure we have understood the specific questions with which a person is honestly struggling. An appreciation of individual personality differences can help us better understand another person, the nature of that person's struggles, and what a helpful response might be.

Whether at home, at work, in the congregation, the community, or in the world, one thing is clear. God has graciously gifted every person. Each of us is one of God's gifted people. As Christians, we also know from Christ's example and the rest of the Bible that our gifts were not given to us for us to keep to ourselves. In the discovery of our gifts and the development of our personal giftedness, we are better able to *use* our gifts as a way of saying "thank you" to God—in all areas of our life. When we employ our gifts as God intended us to, then we are responding faithfully to our common call to use our gifts to "equip the saints for the work of ministry" and so build up the body of Christ.

References and Resources

For those who would like to explore related books and materials, some of which have been useful to me in the preparation of this book, I make the following suggestions. Each of these resources has something important to say, either about personality or spirituality or both.

Unfortunately, when it comes to materials in the area of personality and spirituality I have found more than a little chaff along with the wheat. For whatever help it might be, I would like to share with you some of the guidelines I keep in mind as I decide how much I will rely on a particular resource.

When I evaluate a book on spirituality, there are certain questions that I ask. For example:

1. Is the author solidly grounded in a religious tradition? What is it? Knowing what an author believes helps me understand what that author assumes to be true, but what I might need a little more explanation if I am to understand.

2. Does the author not only *know* about spirituality, but also seem to be a spiritual person? I especially value those who are clearly speaking out of the depths of personal experience.

3. Does the author seem open to *other* ways people can express their faithfulness or does the author assume there only one "right" way?

4. How does the author understand spirituality? Is spirituality only a *part* of life or is spirituality at the *heart* of life, imparting meaning to everything else?

5. What does the author think makes for a spiritual person? Do people become spiritual by doing certain things in a certain way? Does the author suggest that we become whole by climbing some spiritual ladder to God? I listen more carefully to those who counsel me not to trust in myself, but to trust in a loving and gracious God who is revealed in Jesus Christ.

When it comes to an author's perspective on personality, I have other questions that I ask. Since we have been using the Myers-Briggs Type Indicator, I will limit my comments to those who write books or other resources about the MBTI and its applications:

1. What is the author's training and experience that would qualify him or her as an expert in the MBTI? Consulting Psychologists Press limits access to the MBTI to psychologists and others who have had formal course work in interpreting tests and measurements, or the equivalent. Has the author had that kind of training? One of the reasons for such a requirement is that all psychological instruments have strengths and limitations. Trained people recognize what can and cannot be done with the MBTI.

2. Beyond a general understanding of tests and measurements, what is the author's training and experience with the MBTI itself? As a faculty member both for the Center for Applications of Psychological Type and the Association for Psychological Type, I have become aware that many claim expertise in the use of MBTI without having had the kind of training that I believe is basic.

3. Does the author realize how important it is for persons to have an accurate idea of their true personality type? Some authors offer ways other than the MBTI to

determine your type. Is their substitute a valid and reliable method? Does the author give you guidance on the limitations of the substitute approach? If we are misled in identifying our personality gifts, then we may rely on a gift that is not ours, or neglect a gift that is.

4. Does one or more personality types come through as being better or more desirable than the others? If the author is adequately trained in the MBTI, then there will be no Type bias. All personality types are gifts of God.

5. Is personality type being used inappropriately to exclude people or to say that a person cannot do something because that person has the "wrong" personality type? A person is more than Type. With motivation, and certainly with God, even "impossible" things become possible. The four letters of the MBTI are not meant to close down those possibilities, but to open them up to that person and to the rest of God's people.

While some of the following materials are stronger than others, keeping my guidelines in mind should help you recognize any limitations. I think you can find something of value in each of the following resources:

Franz, Marie–Louise von, and James Hillman. *Lectures on Jung's Typology.* Irving, TX: Spring Publications, 1971.

Grant, W. Harold, M. Thompson, and T. Clarke. *From Image to Likeness: A Jungian Path in the Gospel Journey.* New York: Paulist Press, 1983.

Harbaugh, Gary L. *The Faith-hardy Christian.* Minneapolis: Augsburg, 1986.

Harbaugh, Gary L. *Pastor as Person.* Minneapolis: Augsburg, 1984.

Hartzler, Margaret, and Gary Hartzler. *Using Type with Couples.* 1988. Published and distributed by Type Resources, Inc., 101 Chestnut St. #135, Gaithersburg, MD 20877.

Hirsh, Sandra K. *Using the Myers–Briggs Type Indicator in Organizations.* Palo Alto, CA: Consulting Psychologists Press (CPP), 1985.

Hirsh, Sandra K. and Jean M. Kummerow. *Introduction to Type in Organizational Settings*. Palo Alto, CA: CPP, 1987.

Hirsh, Sandra K. and Jean Kummerow. *LIFETypes*. New York: Warner Books, Inc., 1989.

Jung, Carl Gustav. *Psychological Types*. Princeton: Princeton University Press, 1971 (orig. ed. 1923).

Lawrence, Carolyn M., Ann W. Galloway, and Gordon D. Lawrence. *Practice Centers Approach to Seatwork: A Handbook*. Gainesville, FL: CAPT, 1988.

Lawrence, Gordon D. *People Types and Tiger Stripes: A Practical Guide to Learning Styles*, 2nd ed. Gainesville, FL: CAPT, 1982.

Limburg, James. *Psalms for Sojourners*. Minneapolis: Augsburg, 1987.

McCaulley, Mary H. *Jung's Theory of Psychological Types and the Myers–Briggs Type Indicator*. Gainesville, FL: CAPT, 1981.

Myers, Isabel Briggs. *Introduction to Type*. Rev. ed. Palo Alto: CPP, 1987.

Myers, Isabel Briggs, and Mary H. McCaulley. *Manual: A Guide to the Development and Use of the Myers–Briggs Type Indicator*. Palo Alto: CPP, 1985.

Myers, Isabel Briggs, with Peter Myers. *Gifts Differing*. Palo Alto: CPP, 1980.

Nuechterlein, Ann Marie. *Improving Your Multiple Staff Ministry*. Minneapolis: Augsburg, 1989.

Olbert, Scott. "Reducing Warfare over Worship." *Lutheran Partners*. May/June 1987, pp. 16-20. See also Gary L. Harbaugh. "A Few Clarifications." *Lutheran Partners*. Sept./Oct. 1987, pp. 6-7.

Oswald, Roy M., and Otto Kroeger. *Psychological Type and Religious Leadership*. Washington, D.C.: Alban Publications, 1987.

Page, Earle C. "Finding and Following Your Spiritual Path." Gainesville, FL: CAPT.

Page, Earle C. *Looking at Type: A Description of the Preferences Reported by the Myers–Briggs Type Indicator*. Gainesville, FL: CAPT, 1983.

Provost, Judith A. *A Casebook: Applications of the Myers–Briggs Type Indicator in Counseling*. Gainesville, FL: CAPT, 1984.

Provost, Judith A., and Scott Anchors. *Applications of the Myers–Briggs Type Indicator in Higher Education*. Palo Alto, CA: CPP, 1987.

Quenk, A. P., and Naomi Quenk. "The Use of Psychological Typology in Analysis." In *Jungian Analysis*, edited by M. Stein. LaSalle, IL: Open Court Press, 1982.

Quenk, Alex T. *Psychological Types and Psychotherapy.* Gainesville, FL: CAPT, 1985.

Rollins, Wayne G. *Jung and the Bible.* Atlanta: John Knox Press, 1983.

Tagliaferre, Lewis, and Gary L. Harbaugh. *Recovery from Loss.* Deerfield Beach, FL: Health Communications, Inc., 1990.

Taylor, Walter F. *Ephesians.* Minneapolis: Augsburg, 1985.

Yeakley, Flavil, Jr., ed. *The Discipling Dilemma.* Nashville: Gospel Advocate, 1988.

To keep current on MBTI resources, I recommend that you periodically write to the Center for Applications of Psychological Type (CAPT, 2720 N.W. 6th St., Gainesville FL 32609), the Association for Psychological Type (APT, P.O. Box 5099, Gainesville FL 32602), and Consulting Psychologists Press (CPP, 577 College Ave., Palo Alto CA 94306). CPP publishes a professional catalog, APT members receive the *Journal of Psychological Type* and the *Bulletin of Psychological Type,* and CAPT distributes a wide range of reading materials on psychological type and publishes annually a free catalog of MBTI resources. Some of the titles CAPT carried in the most recent catalog include: *Jung and the Christian Way; Cherishing Our Differences; One of a Kind; It Takes All Types; Type Talk; Type and Teamwork; The Myers–Briggs Type Indicator and Leadership; Leadership Equation; The Myers–Briggs Type Indicator and the Teaching–Learning Process; Psychological Type Differences in Education; A Teacher's Guide to Type; Procrastination: Using Psychological Type Concepts to Help Students; Introduction to Temperament; Sixteen Types; Learning Patterns & Temperament Styles; A Parent's Guide to Type; Questions Children May Have about Type Differences; Prayer and Temperament; Prayer and Different Types of People; and Portraits of Temperament.* The guidelines on pages 108-109 can help you evaluate the potential usefulness of these resources.

How to Use This Book: Applications for Personal Growth

A book serves only part of its purpose if it is interesting. *God's Gifted People* was written so that it would also make a *difference* in your daily life.

To help you make that difference, this section offers additional ways to use the material in *God's Gifted People*. Applications are included for your personal life and your relationships at home, at school, at work, and as a member of a congregation. The chapters of this book themselves provide some help in these areas, so what you will find here are additional questions and ideas. Using the headings at the top of the pages that follow, you can quickly identify the areas of growth that are of the most interest to you.

You can read through these applications alone, but many people appreciate having the opportunity to think about new ideas in a small study group, adult class, or as part of a continuing education event. However, even if you use these pages in a group setting, it is suggested that you first take the time to write down your initial, *personal* responses in the space provided.

This edition of *God's Gifted People* also adds an index of key words. The index will make it easier for you to locate the places in the book that you especially want to find (or find again).

With these additional helps, my hope is that *God's Gifted People* will be a book that you will want to go back to from time to time to see if there are any changes for you. I hope it will also be a book that you will want to recommend to a family member or friend.

Personal Growth

In the order of their meaningfulness to you (#1 is most meaningful to you; #4 is least meaningful; there should be no "ties"), rank the following:

_____ PHYSICAL   _____ EMOTIONAL

_____ MENTAL   _____ SOCIAL

Looking up these words in the index will help you see why each of the personality types tends to rank the physical, mental, emotional, and social dimensions in a different order. Even if they were to rank them similarly, the different personality types probably would have different *reasons* for giving the same rank to one of the dimensions. For example, an Extravert might rank SOCIAL as #1 because, for the Extravert, energy comes from the outside world. However, a Feeling type might rank SOCIAL as #1 because of the importance of interpersonal relationships to a Feeling type. Typically, Sensing types usually rank the physical higher than Intuitive types do. Thinking types usually rank the mental above the emotional, and Feeling types generally rank the emotional higher than the mental. The social is usually ranked higher by Extraverts than by Introverts and higher by Feeling types than by Thinking types. Once in a while an introverted Thinking type will rank the social as #1. But this ranking probably has less to do with personality type than with that person's individual history, life circumstance, or work situation.

In what ways does your ranking reflect what might be typical for your personality type? In what ways does your ranking *not* reflect what is typical?

If your ranking is *not* typical for your personality type, what *other* than personality type helps you account for the way you ranked these four dimensions? If you are "going against the grain" (responding in a way not typical for one with your personality gifts), describe how you deal with the energy drain that going against the grain involves.

Your ranking may be pretty much in the order that one would expect for your personality type, and you may feel quite comfortable with your preferences. Sometimes, however, being comfortable with our preferences means that the dimensions we do *not* prefer are *neglected*. Of the four dimensions, which one are *you* most likely to neglect? Since each of the four dimensions is important in experiencing the fullness of God's creation, what growth steps could you take to maintain a healthy (and faithful) balance of the physical, mental, emotional, and social dimensions of life?

Notice that the SPIRITUAL is not to be ranked along with the physical, mental, emotional, and social. In my book *The Faith-hardy Christian*, I show how, in the Bible, the spiritual is not just a *part* of life, but at the *center* of all of life. However, people with different personality gifts are likely to view the spiritual as being more connected with *one* of the four dimensions than with the others. In which of the four dimensions (physical, mental, emotional, and social) are *you* most likely to see God at work? How does your personality gift contribute to your ability to recognize the presence and power of the Spirit in that dimension?

Applications for Couples

Chapter 7 (pp. 90-99) shows you how to use personality type preferences to understand close personal relationships. The chapter summarizes how communication, decision making, intimacy, and other issues are viewed by persons with different personality preferences. Looking at the list on page 93, which of the "problem spots" for couples has been a problem for you?

From this list of issues, identify one *recent* difference of opinion between you and your spouse (or "significant other") where personality preferences seem to have been involved.

Identify one *long-standing* difference between you and your spouse (or "significant other") that might be explained at least in part by differences in personality type.

It is possible that you and your partner have exactly the same personality type preferences. That is not usually the case, though, since the research seems to suggest that most people marry someone with one or two *different* personality preferences. However, since no combination of two types is necessarily incompatible, a more relevant question is what are the specific *challenges* (problems and possibilities) that you as a couple face. If all of your personality type preferences are the same, describe how you as a couple handle the responsibilities that are usually easier for opposite types. For example, Sensing Judging (SJ) types usually pay more attention to specific facts and related tasks, such as checkbook recording and remembering important calendar dates. If you and your "significant other" are both Intuitive Perceptives (NP), as a couple you (or at least one of you) would have to pay close attention to "SJ" areas or some things might not get done. Where you and your partner have the same preferences, discuss what aspects of your relationship are most likely to get overlooked and what might be necessary to improve the situation.

There are certain values in a relationship, such as fidelity and trust, that are not explainable on the basis of personality preferences. This is because a value like fidelity is less related to preference than to the presence or absence of an underlying commitment. However, many of the other things that couples argue about are more likely to create serious and long-lasting conflict if the couple confuses their individual personality preferences with what is the "right" thing to do. Christian couples can further complicate these differences by claiming that one position is "good" and the opposite point of view is "bad" or "sinful." The value of identifying an area of conflict as a difference in preference is that it is easier to reach a compromise about preferences than when one position is perceived as fundamentally *right* and the other as fundamentally *wrong*. As a couple, identify one or two conflict areas that you have in the past viewed as a "right vs. wrong" issue that also might be explained as a difference in personality preferences. How could you reach a satisfying compromise in that area if it is really a matter of *preference* rather than a question of right or wrong?

Love is understood differently by different personality types. What one partner may think is a loving thing to do may not be *perceived* as loving by the other partner. For example, an Extravert may think it loving to keep up a constant flow of communication, sharing ideas and feelings as they arise, while an introverted partner may really prefer to have more times of quiet or at least times without too many interruptions. Each of the other preferences for Sensing or Intuition, Thinking or Feeling, Judging or Perceiving also have different ways of loving or feeling loved. Looking at your personality preferences and those of your partner, how can an understanding of personality type help you to love your partner *in your partner's type*? In other words, in a way that a person with your partner's personality type feels especially appreciated? (See Chapter 6, p. 97, for an example of loving "in type" by learning to listen in a different way.)

What might you want or need from your partner for you to feel loved in a way that persons with your personality gifts especially appreciate?

Applications for Families

If you are a parent, grandparent, or friend of a very small child, a primary way to apply your understanding of biblical giftedness and personality type is to appreciate the uniqueness of that child. Those parents who do not know about personality types and the equal value of opposite personality gifts are more likely to confuse their *values* with their personal *preferences*. As a result, thinking they are imparting values to their children, they, in fact, impose their own personal *preferences* onto their children in such a way as to suggest that the parents' preferences are the only "right" or "good" ways to be. While there are some exceptions, most parents (if they do not realize that different personality preferences are gifts from God) will naturally try to help their children be more like themselves. Unfortunately, if an Introvert is born into a family of Extraverts, the family can put great pressure on that introverted child to act in an extraverted way. Not only does this produce stress, but it may even make it harder for the introverted child to realize what his or her personality gift really is, even after the child grows up.

When you were growing up, what kind of family messages did you get that affirmed your personality gifts? What messages, if any, showed that your parents or your family may not have understood your personality as a gift?

Remember, unless a person has taken the standard form of the Myers–Briggs Type Indicator (currently, Form G) *and* that person has verified the results, it is not wise to assume you know what a person's personality preferences are. Both Introverts and Extraverts may come across at home, on the job, or in group activities quite differently from the way they truly are inside. This is particularly true of Introverts. For this reason it may be inaccurate and unfair to assume from outward behavior that you know a person's true personality type. However, if you think of the impression you have of someone as a *possibility* rather than a conclusion, what you "see" in another person can be helpful to raise questions such as, I wonder if my father was an Introvert? If he was, how could that help me better understand some of the ways he communicated with me and went about things when I was growing up?

In the space below, write down whether you think the personality preferences of the various members of your immediate family were E or I, S or N, T or F, J or P. If your guesses are correct, how would this help you understand how you were raised?

Mother:

Father:

Brothers:

Sisters:

Others:

If you are married or in a close relationship, think about your partner's family of origin and do the same for each of those persons (mother, father, brothers, sisters, others):

As you think about the past, you can become aware of how important your personal history is in how you were shaped as a person. An Introvert raised by extraverted parents may have felt the pressure to be an Extravert and may, in fact, have developed excellent skills in extraversion. But that does not change the fact that the Introvert's personality gift is introversion and will remain so throughout life. If you are a parent (or have a relationship with children) now, how can you affirm the God-given personality gifts of your children so that they will not grow up thinking they need to be different than they are in order to be acceptable?

Write the names of your children below. Then write down the kind of affirmation that you think each needs, based on what you think that child's personality gift is. (Remember never to *label* your child or anyone else's. Personality preferences take a while to develop fully and there is no way to know for sure what a child's personality type *truly* is. As you write down the names of your children—or grandchildren, or students—just make a tentative guess as to what their personality gifts *might* be.)

Applications in School

The gifts identified in chapters 3–6 (practicality, personal help-fulness, possibilities for people, and the gift of looking ahead) are presumed to be present at birth—present at least as gift *potentials*. If a young child grows up in an affirming environment, that child's gifts develop quite naturally and easily. However, each of the gifts involves a special way of "seeing," or taking in information, and a special way of deciding what to do with what one sees. School-age children who *take in* information the way a primary school teacher *gives out* information will have an advantage.

Gordon Lawrence, a professor of education, has written or coauthored several books (including *People Types and Tiger Stripes*) in which he identifies the primary ways that different "types" of students learn. Judith Provost and Scott Anchors have also written about the Myers–Briggs and education, but have focused on higher education. These books are recommended if you have a special interest in educational applications (see the bibliography for publication information). You should also know that there is now the Murphy–Meisgeier Type Indicator for Children that can be used with students in grades 2–8. The Myers–Briggs Type Indicator is not appropriate for young children because the MBTI requires approximately an eighth grade reading level and studies show the MBTI is more reliable with adults than with younger persons. More information about these and other educational applications is available from the Center for Applications of Psychological Type (CAPT) and Consulting Psychologists Press (CPP).

Since personality type develops gradually and it is not always possible to know what a younger child's true gifts are, it is probably wiser to think about yourself as you answer the following questions. Then you might think about the possible implications of your answers as they might apply to persons with gifts differing from yours—perhaps your children, your friends, or your students.

You might reread the descriptions of Sensing and Intuition on page 24. The preference for Sensing is different from the preference for Intuition in that persons who have the gift of Sensing usually like to learn new information in a step-by-step manner, with attention to relevant facts. Intuitives, on the other hand, prefer to have the "big picture" before dealing with specifics. In contrast to the sequential learning of the Sensing types, Intuitives are what are sometimes called "global" learners. They also tend to leap ahead of where the teacher is, especially if the teacher is teaching in a Sensing, step-by-step way. If the teacher is an Intuitive, however, a Sensing student may not see how the teacher arrived at a certain conclusion if the teacher does not point out the connections that link the starting point to that conclusion.

As you reflect on your experience in school, was your learning style more Sensing or more Intuitive? Was that because of your natural gift or because that is what the school environment demanded?

When you think of those teachers or classes where you had the greatest difficulty, how do you think your difficulty might be related to your personality type (Extravert or Introvert, Sensing or Intuitive, Thinking type or Feeling type, judging type or Perceiving type; see descriptions on pages 23-26)?

Did you like learning "on your own" or learning in discussion or brainstorming groups? Were you more comfortable in library research or in settings where you could interact with others and discover what you thought by talking about the subject with others? How do you think your learning style was influenced by your preference for Extraversion or Introversion, for Thinking or Feeling?

Sometimes a parent will know about personality types, but a school teacher may not. Also, some teachers may insist on teaching their subject a certain way regardless of the difficulty that approach may create for some of the students. Therefore if you have a school-age child, it is possible that the only way your child may improve will be if she or he can adapt to the teacher's teaching style. As an example of how this might be done, what if an eighth-grade child gifted as an Introverted, Intuitive, Feeling, Judging type (INFJ) had a teacher who seemed to be an Extraverted, Sensing, Thinking, Judging type (ESTJ)? Would an extraverted teacher more likely emphasize class participation or individual desk work? Would a Sensing teacher be inclined to value specific data or general theories? When you think about what might be the preferences of an ESTJ teacher, how could you help your child improve the chances that his or her performance in class (both oral and written work) would be graded more favorably by that teacher?

If you are a Cub Scout or Brownie leader or a Sunday school teacher, how could you adjust your leadership or teaching approach to the variety of gifts represented by those you serve? Think of something you have taught someone else and list below how you might have taught it differently if the person you were teaching were an:

Extravert instead of an Introvert:

Sensing type instead of an Intuitive type:

Thinking type instead of a Feeling type:

Judging type instead of a Perceiving type:

Applications on the Job

There are a number of important ways you can use an understanding of personality gifts on the job. First, while there is no reason that a person of *any* type should not select whatever kind of work is satisfying, it does seem that different personality types seem to be especially attracted to certain kinds of jobs. In research reported by CAPT, 18 percent of a group of math teachers had preferences for Introversion, Sensing, Thinking, and Judging (ISTJ), while less than 3 percent of those math teachers had the exact opposite preferences (ENFP). Why might math be more appealing to an ISTJ than to an ENFP?

Look back on the work you have done in the past. How does your personality type help you understand why some work was more interesting or appealing to you?

In what ways does your present vocation enable you to use your personality gifts? How does what you are doing now *not* make it easy for you to express all of your gifts?

Many workers report that their greatest stress on the job comes from having to "go against the grain," meaning that they are required to extend themselves in exactly the opposite directions from their natural preferences. An ENFP who has to spend most of the month at the end of the fiscal year auditing accounts in an isolated office where there are no other people would probably find that experience much more stressful than would a person whose preferences are ISTJ. Take a look at what stresses you on the job. How does your stress relate to your personality preferences?

Another application of personality type is for improving staff relationships. In what ways might an Extraverted Feeling type go about relating to other staff members differently from an Introverted Thinking type? Which of the two would probably be most upset by differences of opinion or disharmony among staff members? Which of the two might be able to accept criticism better, and even see criticism as constructive?

If a manager who was gifted as an Intuitive (seeing patterns and possibilities) had a secretary who was a Sensing type (seeing specifics, concrete realities), how might their gifts *complement* each other when it came time for a year-end report? If the manager were a Sensing type and the secretary an Intuitive (with few Sensing skills), in what areas might they have the most problems appreciating each other? Does answering this question help you to understand anything about frustrations *you* might have on the job?

People should not select jobs or change jobs on the basis of personality type alone. Having a certain personality type does not guarantee success on the job; not having a certain personality type does not mean a person cannot succeed on the job. Therefore, what other factors—life experiences, present life situation, religious values, etc.—would you want to be sure to consider in addition to personality type if you were considering a vocational change?

Applications for Congregations

It is an eye-opener to know that every congregation of more than a few people is likely to have some members who have the gift of Practicality, and that other members will have either the gift of Personal Helpfulness or the gift of perceiving Possibilities for People or the gift of Looking Ahead. All personality types are represented!

When congregational members are understood to be gifted differently, then there is no longer the expectation that everyone will contribute to congregational life in exactly the same ways. Based on your present awareness of what your personality gifts are, what are the primary ways that you prefer to use your personality gifts in support of your congregation's mission and ministry?

Many congregational practices or customs are not matters of right or wrong, but rather a matter of preference. Not realizing that, congregations sometimes make one or two preferences the "standard" for everyone else in the congregation. For example, having a worship service that never varies in the order of the service is not a question of right or wrong, since God can be worshiped in many ways. Rather, such invariability is a *preference* that has become *absolutized* for all. Are there any practices in your congregation that seem to be more a matter of preference than of correctness? How welcoming do you think your congregation appears to persons who have the exact opposite preferences of what has been "standardized" in your congregation?

Which of the personality gifts seems to be more prominent in your congregation, the gift of Practicality, Personal Helpfulness, Possibilities for People, or the gift of Looking Ahead? How does this prominence affect the priorities in your congregation? Which of these four gifts seems to be *least* evident in your congregation? As a result, what areas of ministry are less likely to be developed?

Review the "Spiritual" sections of each of the four gift chapters (pages 43-44, 57-58, 69-70, 82-83), the definitions of the different personality preferences (pages 23-26), and chapter 7, pages 99-104. What could be done so that worship in your congregation would be equally appealing to each of God's gifted people? If only personality type were involved, what do you think the worship preferences of these people would be:

Extraverts

Introverts

Sensing types

Intuitive types

Thinking types

Feeling types

Judging types

Perceiving types

Applications for Evangelism

Evangelism is the sharing of the good news of the gospel. While the good news of what God has done in Christ Jesus is a singular message, the Pentecost experience reminds us that the gospel is more likely to be heard if it is communicated in the language of the hearer (Acts 2:1-11). One of the ways to use an understanding of personality types is to realize that each type has a "language" of its own.

What we commonly mean when we use the word *evangelism* today is a congregation's outreach to prospective or inactive members. This may be understood as a way of attracting people into the life of a congregation so that those persons can hear the gospel and discover in an ongoing way the gospel's relevance to their lives.

To make the church's evangelism efforts in this regard more effective, *God's Gifted People* can be used to think about how an invitation might need to be initially presented to a prospective member who has, for example, the gift of practicality. Would á different way of phrasing the invitation be helpful if instead of the gift of *practicality* that prospective member had the personality gift of *possibilities*? In the course of growth to Christian maturity, the gospel must be proclaimed as it relates both to practicalities and to possibilities. But the *initial* presentation is more likely to be heard if it is in the "language" of the person who is hearing it. After reviewing chapter 3, you will see that persons with the gift of practicality combine a preference for taking in information by means of Sensing (concrete and specific data) and for making decisions on the basis of a logical analysis of the facts. To attract a person who has the God-given gift of Practicality, what information about a congregation and its priorities would need to be included in making an initial contact?

What would be the primary things about a congregation that a prospective member would want to know if that prospective member had:

The gift of Personal Helpfulness (chapter 4):
The gift of Possibilities for People (chapter 5):
The gift of Looking Ahead (chapter 6):

Attracting a person to a congregation is only part of the task of evangelism. That new person must also be assimilated into the congregation and helped to make a contribution that goes beyond the giving of money. There is probably a similarity between what attracts a person to a congregation and what that person might find most appealing as an area of personal involvement. Using the information that helped you to answer the question immediately above, what kinds of contributions would the following probably be interested in making?

Persons whose gift is Living in the Here and Now (chapter 3):

Persons whose gift is Reaching Out and Lifting Up (chapter 4):

Persons whose gift is Keeping Hope Alive (chapter 5):

Persons whose gift is Letting the Future Guide the Present (chapter 6):

Applications for Stewardship

There is a connection between evangelism and stewardship. Each of us has been given a gift that we are intended to use not only for ourselves but also for others. Stewardship efforts are best understood as opportunities to *help* people to give their gifts. However, stewardship activities are often too narrowly focused, appealing primarily only to one or two of the personality types. Just as in evangelism, stewardship appeals need to be communicated in the various "languages" spoken by those with differing gifts.

Which of the personality types do you think might be most responsive to "temple talks" that highlight current deficits and building maintenance needs (whether for money contributions or for contributing personal time)? Why?

Which of the personality types might see more opportunity to give their gifts as a result of a discussion group focusing on the needs of the homeless or the possibility of the congregation opening a "community kitchen"? Why?

Which of the personality types might respond best not to a personal visit or a group discussion, but simply to a well-reasoned letter presenting a global mission issue? Why?

In addition to temple talks, many congregations utilize every-member visits or "cottage meetings." Evaluate these and the other kinds of stewardship appeals made in your congregation from the standpoint of which personality types are more likely to find these appeals "appealing."

Applications for Social Ministry

Social ministry is an application that we also considered in relationship to stewardship (persons, groups, or congregations ministering to the homeless or opening a community kitchen). Social ministry committees also may deal with the long-range consequences of local and national political policies and the ethical dilemmas those policies may create. While people may have opinions that are based on things other than their Myers–Briggs preferences, personality gifts are usually in some way involved in which aspects of a social concern are considered most important. After reviewing the descriptions on pages 23-26 and recalling the differences between the ST, SF, NF, and NT combinations, what strengths do you think each of the combinations brings to a discussion of such broad social ministry issues as the homeless, AIDS, abortion, divestment, sexism or racism, or other situations where injustice may be involved? Since each of these areas may draw on the personality preferences in a different way, it probably will be easier to select just one of the areas of social ministry listed above as you consider the strengths brought to that discussion by those gifted with ST, SF, NF, and NT.

For every *strength* in being able to see things a certain way, there is a corresponding *limitation* in not being able to see equally well from the opposite point of view. Take another one of the issues above and give your opinion of how persons with differing personality gifts might work most effectively together toward resolution of that issue in a way that respects the perspective of each.

Applications for Mission and Inclusivity

There was a time when one of the major Protestant denominations made appeals for world mission support by including world missions in the general benevolence of the church. Many people found this less persuasive than when the denomination identified specific missionaries in specific places in the world who had specific needs—missionaries whom the congregation could "adopt" as they helped to fill those needs. In what ways does an understanding of personality type explain the differences in the effectiveness of these two types of appeals?

In the efforts of the church to be more inclusive, whether in local congregations or in its global outlook, an understanding of differing personality gifts may be of help. Jung believed that all "types" of persons are found in all nations of the world. While personal life history, culture, and current life situation affect the *expression* of personality type, it is reasonable to assume that persons with one type of personality gift will have something very much in common with persons of another gender or socioeconomic group or culture who have that same personality gift. Describe any experiences you have had where having a similar personality type may have helped you to relate to someone with a very different background from yours.

How could an appreciation of God-given personality gifts, each of which has counterparts in persons of different cultures, contribute to a greater feeling of sisterhood and brotherhood throughout the world?

Applications for Property Committees

It is probable that the majority of persons who are interested in and serve on property committees are Sensing types. Persons with a Sensing gift are ordinarily quicker to notice the need for repair or replacement and tend to value the physical and material more highly than Intuitives. However, the support of Intuitives for building and renovation projects is very important. Using the descriptions on pp. 23-26, what might be the most effective ways of helping persons of differing personality types to appreciate the need for improvement of existing property or for additional building?

To appeal to Extraverts:

To appeal to Introverts:

To appeal to Intuitives:

To appeal to Thinking types:

To appeal to Feeling types:

To appeal to Judging types:

To appeal to Perceiving types:

Applications for Women of the Church

There is one gender difference in estimates of the way that personality gifts are distributed. Women are thought to be approximately 60 percent Feeling types, whereas men are thought to be approximately 60 percent Thinking types. Whether as individuals or in women's organizations or general congregational activities, it therefore appears that the female voice and the male voice are needed complements of one another in the congregation.

Review the characteristics of the Thinking preference and of the Feeling preference (p. 25). Identify the ways that the Thinking and Feeling preferences can work together for the good of all in the following challenges that congregations sometimes face:

Resolving a conflict among church members:

Deciding on budget priorities at a congregational meeting:

Deciding on whether or not to take on a congregational project, such as sponsoring a refugee family:

In planning and presenting programs for women of the church, what content choices and presentation methods would ensure that the program would be of equal interest to women with the differing gifts of ST (Practicality), SF (Personal Helpfulness), NF (Possibilities for People), and NT (Looking Ahead)?

Applications for Men of the Church

Since the one gender difference on the Myers–Briggs is the difference between males and females on the Thinking–Feeling scale (with approximately 60 percent of males preferring Thinking), it is understandable that many men's groups in congregations have, as their reason to meet, a *common task* (Thinking types are usually more task oriented than relationship oriented). As you look back over the history of men's groups in your congregation, have those groups flourished more when there was a goal to meet than when the group was primarily for social purposes?

What kinds of tasks or goals does your congregation have that might benefit from the united efforts of a men's group?

Since growth in the Spirit is not only through what we do, but also by affirming and appreciating who we are (and whose we are), how could an understanding of differing personality gifts help men appreciate themselves and each other, and also appreciate more fully the complementary gifts that gender differences bring?

Some research suggests that in mid-life, males (predominantly Thinking types) get more in touch with their Feeling side. Have you noticed this in anyone you know? Do persons *lose* themselves by allowing more of a place for the opposite gifts, or does a person *grow* when they are open to the opposites? How and why?

Applications for Pastors, Pastoral Relations Committees, and Recruitment of Persons for Full-time Ministry

For those congregations who have the opportunity to select their pastors, an understanding of personality type can be very useful. *However, there is one major caution that must be reemphasized.* You cannot tell whether or not a pastor will be a good pastor by what four Myers–Briggs letters the pastor has! For one thing, having a personality type preference does not mean that a pastor is good at it! Because a pastor (or any other person) prefers Extraversion does not automatically make that pastor a skilled Extravert. On the other hand, even if the pastor has a personality gift for Introversion, that does not mean that the pastor *cannot* be skilled in extraverting! So, to select a pastor on the basis of a type preference (or to exclude someone from consideration because that pastor has the "wrong" preferences) would be a terrible misuse of personality type. As a matter of fact, God may have called a pastor to serve the congregation who has what some consider to be the "wrong" MBTI letters, but who God knows is exactly the right person for the ministry challenges that exist!

However, it *is* an appropriate use of personality type theory to indicate to prospective pastors the kinds of needs that the congregation has that *any* pastor, regardless of personal preferences, would want and need to know about. That kind of information could help a prospective pastor discern whether or not to accept a call to the congregation and, if so, how to use (and supplement) the pastor's own personality gifts in order to serve that parish more effectively.

As you think about your congregation, what kinds of personality skills is it important for your pastor to have?

(Remember, a pastor can be *skilled* in a personality preference, even if that is not the pastor's *gift*.)

Pastors who are introverted usually do not show their "best" personality gifts as quickly as pastors who are extraverted. This is because Extraverts use their dominant or best gift in their favorite world, which is the outer world of people and things. Introverts are more likely to use their dominant gift in the inner world and usually share their inner world with others only after they get to know them well. As a result, extraverted pastors usually make a better early impression than introverted pastors. Have you known pastors who fit the extraverted pattern? Any whom you think were Introverts who shared their inner world more slowly?

How would you help an introverted pastor to feel welcome and appreciated during the first weeks after the pastor's arrival? What would be important welcoming signs for an extraverted pastor?

One of the responsibilities of a congregation is to identify persons who should be encouraged to attend seminary in preparation for full-time ministry, whether as an ordained person or as a lay minister. Since there is no one personality type that makes a more effective and faithful minister, the Myers–Briggs Type Indicator cannot be helpful for that purpose. However, there are certain interpersonal and leadership skills that are needed in ministry. What kinds of gifts or skills would suggest to you that a person should be encouraged to consider full-time service in the church?

Applications for Multiple Staff Ministries

Just as in selecting a pastor, it would be inappropriate to select staff members on the basis of their Myers–Briggs results. As noted earlier, having a preference does not mean that one is capable in the use of it; not having a particular preference, such as extraversion, does not mean that the person cannot be highly skilled in it. Therefore, personality type preferences are neither a reliable nor a fair way of selecting *or* excluding a potential staff person from consideration for a position. However, *after* staff persons are selected it is helpful to look at the staff makeup from the standpoint of personality preferences and to give some thought to how the full range of personalities found in the congregation can best be served.

If you are in a congregation that has a staff ministry, what range of personality gifts (chapters 3–6) seem to be represented by those staff persons? (Remember, a staff person has only one of these as a *gift*, although a person may be *skilled* in all of them.)

The gift of Practicality:

The gift of Personal Helpfulness:

The gift of Possibilities for People:

The gift of Looking Ahead:

If you had an opportunity to add a staff member, along with that person's personality gifts, would your congregation benefit more from that staff member having an especially well-developed *skill* in (1) practicality, (2) personal helpfulness, (3) possibilities for people, or (4) looking ahead so the future can guide the present? Why and how?

Applications for Church Denominations and Judicatories (conferences, synods/dioceses/presbyteries, etc.)

Not only individuals within a congregation, but congregations themselves can have a predominant "personality." Do you think your congregation primarily expresses the gift of (1) practicality, (2) personal helpfulness, (3) possibilities for people, or (4) looking ahead to let the future guide the present?

Do you think your *denomination* primarily expresses the gift of (1) practicality, (2) personal helpfulness, (3) possibilities for people, or (4) looking ahead to let the future guide the present?

If your congregation (or denomination) needed to express any personality gift more than what it does now, which of the gifts would you hope it would be: (1) practicality, (2) personal helpfulness, (3) possibilities for people, or (4) the gift of looking ahead and letting the future guide the present?

How would this additional expression make your congregation (denomination) more effective and faithful in mission and ministry?

Applications for Ecumenical and Interfaith Relations

It is possible that, in addition to theological convictions, one of the other reasons different communities of faith developed was so that there would be greater opportunity to express certain of the personality gifts. In fact, some of the denominations appear to be more practically oriented while others appear to be more possibility oriented. Some are more focused on personal helpfulness in the present and others on broader programmatic programs that address anticipated problems of the future. How can an understanding of personality gifts (and denominational gifts) lead to an increased appreciation for the value of ecumenical relationships?

If you broaden your perspective and think not only about other Christian denominations but also about other world religions, how could Christians best use their differing gifts to maintain open dialogue with those of another faith?

When you look at the world as a whole, including past events and future possibilities, what do you think God intended in choosing to gift us differently?

Other Applications

What an understanding of differing personality gifts does is make it possible for us to ask some new questions about many of the things we usually take for granted. One example is intelligence. We assume that we know what intelligence means and that it can be measured with an IQ test. However, if people are gifted differently, then perhaps there are *different kinds* of intelligence—only some of which are measured by "intelligence" tests currently available. It may also be that currently available tests actually favor certain kinds of intelligence over others. If so, then we need to be careful before concluding that we can compare the intelligence level of different people simply by comparing their IQ scores! Is it possible that teachers would be able to assess the potential of children more accurately if they were more familiar with what can be learned from a Myers–Briggs approach to "giftedness"? Books such as *Gifts Differing* and *People Types and Tiger Stripes* help us raise these and other relevant questions about education.

The same kinds of questions can be raised about many other areas. I currently offer programs and workshops on the following: personality gifts and relationships; love and sexuality; marriage and family life; stress; health and wholeness; crisis; preretirement; death and dying and other loss experiences; teamwork in staff and committee relationships; faith-hardiness; spirituality; and a variety of other "person in ministry" issues (whether ordained ministry or the ministry of the laity). In addition, I bring the perspective of personality gifts into my Kairos Care and Counseling℠ work with individuals, couples, and families and into my consultation work with congregations and judicatories of the church.

This is not to say that a perspective on personality gifts or the Jungian/Myers–Briggs way of looking at life is the answer (with a capital A) in all these areas. It is a helpful perspective, but it is not the *only* perspective and, as emphasized in *God's Gifted People*, we are much more as persons than any four (or four thousand!) letters could possibly indicate. God has created us in all our marvelous complexity—a complexity that goes beyond what any test or measurement or indicator can fully comprehend. However, you should find it enlightening to use a personality gift/Myers–Briggs way of looking at common, everyday occurrences. One recent book, *LIFETypes*, does this in terms of Living, Learning, Laboring, Leading, Leisure, Loving, and Losing Out. My earlier work, *The Faith-hardy Christian*, applies Myers–Briggs understandings both in daily life and in life transitions involving stress, health problems, role change, loss, conflict, and spiritual questions and concerns.

Requesting a catalog from the Center for Applications of Psychological Type will keep you current with the latest resources and applications being made with the Myers–Briggs. If you have found *God's Gifted People* to be helpful, you will probably be interested in some of the other materials available through CAPT (see References and Resources for additional suggestions and addresses).

Index

This index is provided for your convenience in the event you have certain areas of interest that you would like to look up first, or in case you would like to return to an idea in the book that was especially interesting or helpful.

Each of the applications of personality gifts is identified in this index to make it easier for you to use *God's Gifted People* for yourself, with your family and friends, at work or at school, or in your congregation.

Association for Psychological Type, 22, 108, 111
Assumptions in the book, 11–17
Baptism, 12
Bible: Acts 6:4—88; Acts 20:24—88; 1 Cor. 12—11; 2 Cor. 5:18—89; Deut. 30:19—95; 1 Pet. 4—11; Eph. 3:14-19—100; Eph. 4-11, 47, 88; Jer. 1—21; John 3:16—11; Luke 6:38—48; Matt. 28:19-20—88; Mic. 6:8—88; Phil. 3:13—94; Ps. 118:24—93; Ps. 139—21; Rom. 6:6-14—17; Rom. 7:15-23—17; Rom. 12—11, 88
Briggs, Katherine, 22
Center for Applications of Psychological Type (CAPT), 22, 27, 36, 108, 111
Christ, 11, 100
Choosing life, 95
Community, 13
Conflict, 89–99

Consulting Psychologists Press (CPP), 27, 89, 108, 111
Decision making, 93, 94–96
Education, 43, 58, 70, 83
Emotional, 42, 56–57, 69, 82
ENFJ, 29, 66
ENFP, 29, 65–66
ENTJ, 29, 77
ENTP, 29, 78–79
ESFJ, 28, 52
ESFP, 28, 54
ESTJ, 28, 37, 92–99
ESTP, 28, 38
Extraversion (E), 23–24, 30
Gifts: common good, 15; differing, 13; God as Giver, 15, 16, 21, 22, 46, 98; measure, 12; personality, 17, 18–23; purpose, 16; roles, 12, 13; source, 11; spiritual, 14–15, 45; strengths and limitations, 98; theology, 104–106; unique, 20; varieties, 15
Gifts Differing, 89
God, 15, 16, 21, 22, 46, 98

Index

Gospel, 89
Grace, 15, 16, 17
Greatest gift, 11
Handedness (left and right), 46
History, 17
Inclusive church, 103
Incompatibility, 94
Individual, 13, 15
INFJ, 29, 66–67
INFP, 29, 65, 92–99
INTJ, 29, 77–78
INTP, 29, 78
Innate, 20
Intimacy, 93, 95–96
Introduction to Type, 27
Introversion (I), 22–23, 30, 35
Intuition (N), 24, 31
ISFJ, 28, 52–53
ISFP, 28, 53
ISTJ, 28, 39
ISTP, 28, 38–39
Jesus, 61, 89
Judgment (J), 26, 31, 35
Jung, Carl Gustav, 20–22
Justification, 11
Lawrence, Gordon, 22, 30, 46
Learning, 43, 58, 70, 83
Life situation, 17
Looking ahead, 73–87
Manual (Myers–Briggs), 36
Material possessions, 93
Moses, 94-95
Mental, 42, 56, 68–69, 81–82
Marriage, 90–99; incompatability in, 94; typical problems in, 93–99
Mid-life, 47
Ministry, 89
Mission, 89, 104–106
Myers, Isabel Briggs, 22, 36, 89
Myers, Peter B., 89

Myers–Briggs Type Indicator,[R] 22, 27, 30, 45, 89, 92, 108; limitations of, 40
NF, 61–72
NT, 73–87
Pastoral care, 44, 58
Pastors: ST, 44–45; SF, 58–59; NF, 70–71; NT, 83–84
Paul, the apostle, 11–17, 88
People Types and Tiger Stripes, 22
Perception (P), 24, 32, 35, 94
Personal helpfulness, 49–60
Personhood, 17
Physical, 41, 55–56, 68, 81
Possibilities for people, 61–72
Practicality, 33–48
Psychology, 20, 40
Reconciliation, 89–99, 98
Salvation, 89
Sensing (S), 24–25, 31, 34
Sermons, 43, 57, 69, 82–83
Sexual intimacy, 93, 96
Sin, 17, 98
Skill, 46
Social, 43, 57, 69, 82
Spirit, 20
Spiritual, 43, 57–58, 69–70, 82–83, 99–104
Spiritual expression 100–104
Spirituality, 100, 107–108
SF, 49–60
ST, 33–48, 50
Thinking (T), 25, 31, 34
Tradition, 58, 104
Type, 27
Type table, 27–30
Values, 98
Whole person (Wholeness), 17, 41, 48, 55
Worship, 43, 58, 70, 83, 99, 101–104